WHITE SQUAW

By Dolores Cline Brown

Edited by Jim Rearden

Manufactured in the United States of America

Wolfe Publishing Company
ISBN: 1-879356-13-9

June 1992

Wolfe Publishing Company
6471 Airpark Drive
Prescott, Arizona 86301

Contents

DEDICATION

To Yukon's Na Cho Nyakdun Indian people, for their help and friend-ship, and for the wonderful times we have shared under Northern skies.

Dolores Cline Brown

The Owl, He Talks

The soft swish of snowshoes broke the silence. Our trail was a crinkly ribbon of white that wound between spun-sugar-coated arctic spruce. Feathery tracks of sharptail grouse were the only signs of life. The ominous, booming, hoot of a great horned owl echoed from the deep forest. "Dolores, cover your face. It's more than 50 below," said my broad-shouldered husband, as he looked back. He didn't stop, but continued to swing his snowshoes in rhythmic strides.

"Oh. Louis, I think I'm frosted already." I said, half-frightened. Slipping a hand from a long-furred lynx mitten, I felt my upper lip. Tiny beads of ice were forming. Blowing out my breath, I listened to the faint tinkle of moisture freezing, and watched the ice crystals that my breath had produced slowly drift off.

Louis stopped and rubbed a white spot on my nose. Then he caustically asked, "How in hell did a city girl like you happen to pick the Yukon?" He became rather fierce when he thought I might be suffering.

"Because of an irresistible six-foot man," I laughed.

Louis gave me a grin before swinging back down the trail. I knew his fears. I shared them. I shook the frost from the wolverine ruff around my parka hood, as I tried to shake my growing apprehension. How would I ever survive in this northern wilderness without Louis? What if something happened to him? Wallowing in self-pity, I admitted to myself that sometimes the North terrorized me. However, I had come to love the Yukon. It had been a shock to find that for seven months each year old man winter snapped his lash of arctic storms, and piled ever deeper ice and deep snow. Every creature fights to survive those long frigid months. The soft-furred lynx stalks the unwary snowshoe rabbit; if the lynx wants to live, he must not miss. When the great horned owl swoops silently on a mouse he too must be sure. The snow falls softly, but it forms a prison.

For men and women, there is the solitude. It is peaceful, but all-pervading. The silence is profound. During deep cold of 40 and 50 and even 70 below zero, there may not be even a breeze. Occasionally comes the startling loud crack of forming ice, or the rifle-shot sound from a tree that the squeezing cold has reached.

Then comes spring, glorious, miraculous spring, to unlock the doors of ice. The once-frozen rivers roar with the freedom of breakup, and millions of birds that had vacationed far to the south return, chattering, twittering, whistling, singing. After months of silence, the noise seems deafening—and glorious! I thought longingly of the midnight sun, a warm glowing orb that hovers over wobbly calf moose and playful bear cub. When it arrives, gone is the hunger, the cold, the struggle with the snow and ice, as all creatures bask in its golden warmth.

My snowshoe caught on a root and I sighed, thinking how quickly summer departs. Suddenly, it seems, the sun no longer lights the night. Moose grunt and toss willows with polished antlers. There is a rush of wings as most birds flee south, and once again comes the overwhelming white silence.

Ahead, the spruce trees parted and in a clearing under the mellow moon I could see the amber-colored logs of our little cabin. "Looks like we have company," Louis tossed over his shoulder.

Warm smoke defiantly puffed from our stubby stovepipe. Overhead flares of northern lights writhed as we urged tired legs to lift snowshoes faster. Old Billy DeChuck, our Indian neighbor, flung wide the door. He grinned happily and announced, "Bring four ptarmigan, me."

I hovered over the black-bellied stove after peeling off my parka and gloves. The heat was heavenly. "Billy, it was good of you to light our fire. But how did you know we were coming?"

"Owl, he tell me."

"Owl?" I was puzzled.

Billy nodded his head toward the window, then I heard the low eerie hoot of an owl. It was so close the big bird must have been perched in the spruce tree beside the door. Far in the distance I heard an answering hoot. Our owl gave another hoot.

"What are the owls saying, Billy?"

Billy listened intently, then looked at me. "He say this winter white man he die."

I shuddered. "Maybe you not understand right."

Billy grunted. "What matter with white man? He smart. Why for he not hear owl talk?"

"Maybe it's because he listen too much to radio," I answered.

Billy grunted in agreement. "Radio he no good. Make white man deaf."

Billy reached into his moosehide packsack and hauled out a dark brown mink skin. He chuckled happily as I admired the shiny fur. It took so little to make Billy happy—a fat fish, a plump grouse. Had the white man lost more than he had gained from his civilization?

Louis teased, "You rich man now Billy. You'll get forty-five dollars for that one." Billy shook his head and handed the soft brown fur to me. "You make hat?"

I gasped. "A real mink, for me?" Billy's dusky face beamed. "Sure. Your old man no good. He catch nothing. Billy have to give you mink." We all laughed. Billy was forever running down Louis' trapping ability and bragging about his own.

Billy had so little. I started to refuse the gift. Louis subtly shook his head, and I accepted the mink with many thanks. Louis knew it was important for Billy to be able to share with us. Billy left, glowing with happiness. I knew we would more than repay our wonderful brown-skinned neighbor for his unselfishness.

While moose stew warmed in the cast iron pot, I dashed outside and with flashlight checked the thermometer. Down, down, down, until the sliver of red showed at −54°F. Why did it have to get so cold? Why weren't we ready for winter? I looked at the huge bulk of our unfinished barn. A black cavern yawned where the doors should have been. Winter had arrived before Louis could even get the moss and dirt on the roof poles. Twenty-nine pack and saddle horses we used to take clients on big game hunts huddled inside. Their combined breaths rose in a steamy cloud above the barn roof.

I slammed back inside. "Oh Louis, those poor horses. I don't know how they stand that terrible cold!" Louis pulled on his beaver fur mitts. "Why don't you go out and check on Red while I go up the trail and see why Dora and Dixie didn't show up this morning." I stuffed my pockets with carrots and ran to the barn. Moonlight streamed through an open window. I could see a looming hulk, and as I arrived, a horse whinnied.

"Oh, Red, you're still alive!" There, hanging in a large sling chained to the barn rafters was a dull red horse. He was that rare exception—an animal that never grew a heavy coat of hair in winter. In spite of the thick woolly trapper's blanket Louis had strapped on him, he had collapsed from the cold. It had been a terrible task to get him up. Louis had managed it by improvising a sling, and we had lifted him with a chain hoist. While I pulled the chain, Louis heaved against the horse. Once I looked up and saw Red hanging limp and helpless. I burst into tears.

Louis, gasping for breath, snapped, "Red doesn't need your sympathy. He needs your help. PULL!" I shut my eyes and pulled. After he was safely suspended from the rafters, we rolled in a big drum stove and kept a fire burning in it day and night. Now, after several days, Red seemed to be gaining strength. He nibbled eagerly at the carrots. I buried my face in his mane and my tears ran down his soft warm neck while I lovingly patted him. He looked so pitiful.

"Oh Red, what's going to happen to us? Is the Yukon going to kill us all?"

Back in the cabin I anxiously waited for Louis. When at last he stomped through the door I didn't have to ask. My husband was ready to explode. "Damn those bastards. The wolves killed both of them. They were weak. Not enough hay. In this cold weather they've got to have more hay. I'll go to Dawson City tomorrow for a load."

"Not in this terrible cold. It's a hundred and twenty-five miles," I wailed.

"Can't be helped. It's inhuman to let a horse starve. I'll bet next year I'll cut every damn wild meadow in the Yukon."

"You cut four last fall."

"Not enough. And there's something wrong with the hay."

"How could there be?"

"I've heard old-timers say that the first year you cut a wild meadow, the horses pick up a lot of parasites. Dawson has been raising hay ever since the Klondike gold rush. It's good timothy, and it'll give the horses strength. I'll leave early in the morning."

I lay awake for a long time dreading the morrow, and listening to the occasional sad, deep calls of great horned owls. I fell into a troubled sleep and awoke when my husband bent over the bed to give me a soft good-bye kiss. It was still dark. Northern lights were staining the frost-fern-etched windows with a cathedral glow. Louis had such a nice man smell of warm wool, shaving lotion, and tangy spruce outdoorishness. I clasped my arms around his neck and my heart was bursting with love. Without his strength, his courage, his protection, how could I survive in this fierce land?

4

"I don't want you to go today. You know what the owl told Billy."

Louis snorted. "That damned fool owl. If he had any brains, he'd be up on the mountain where it's warmer."

"But Louis, I had bad dreams."

"What sort of dreams?"

"I hear a knock at the door. I open the door and standing there is a Mounty."

"So you have scarlet fever," Louis teased, giving me a playful spank.

"Please don't joke. He stands there looking so serious. I think he's about to tell me something dreadful."

Louis stood. "You'll have to learn to not let the North bluff you. Remember, you married a trapper and a big game outfitter with a string of hay burners. If I'm to make it to Dawson City and back before night I've got to get going."

"Take your sleeping bag."

"What for? I'll be back tonight."

"I just feel you should take it."

"Dolores, you're going to have to get control of your nerves. If you don't, you'll become as nuts as old Fishhook Ferguson."

"Is it crazy to ask you to take a sleeping bag when it's fifty below zero?" I sniffed, dabbing at my eyes.

Louis slammed out the door. I heard the engine of our one-ton truck. What if the engine stopped and he had nothing to help keep him warm? I didn't know the sharp predawn sting had cooled his temper. He had taken my advice.

I snuggled deeper under the satin-covered down robe. Was wilderness madness creeping up on me? All night I had heard that darned owl hooting. To me it had sounded like he was saying, "Death is on the highway. Death is on the highway." No, I decided, it wasn't madness. My grandfather, old Doc Andrus, was famous throughout the western states for his warning dreams in which the diagnoses of diseases of his patients came to him. Aunt Mae had inherited this penchant for dreams of warning. Now I had a taste of it. But was this a dream of warning?

Candles that Louis had lit before leaving flickered. I glanced about the log cabin and smiled. It seemed so funny for such a small room to serve as kitchen, bedroom, living room, family room, dining room, and foyer. Perhaps still more odd was to see inside the rough-hewn log walls an ornate silver tea set, Spode china, and Louis the 15th furniture—all cherished items from my past life that I had brought to our unlikely union. The beautiful but fragile furniture wasn't up to the rugged wilderness life, for my Louis was wrecking the chairs one by one. He had a habit of sitting violently in a way that was more than the graceful but spindly chairs could handle.

Oh well. They were just things, and they would eventually be replaced by more appropriate and more rugged chairs. I bounced out of bed and counted the money left in the silver teapot. Louis had taken money to pay for hay. Carefully, I counted the worn bills. Only fifty-two dollars! Not much to last until Louis caught a lynx or a mink, or a deposit came from a hunting client for the coming fall big game hunt.

I was restive and uneasy, and hurriedly dressed. I slipped into mukluks and parka and dashed out the door to take Red a carrot. The big horse half swung around and loudly nickered. At the moment he seemed to be my only friend. Copper, a two-year-old colt, so-named because in the sunlight he resembled burnished copper, was, next to Red, my favorite. He shared half of the carrot. Dina, a dappled white mare whose dished face revealed her dash of Arabian blood, nudged me for a bite.

Louis, knowing I needed to be busy during his absence, had asked me to sketch plans for our new home. It would, of course, be built of logs. I was determined to dramatize my remaining French antique furniture with its endearing qualities of familiarity, nostalgia, and, somehow, security. These were assets that would protect me from this wild land.

So engrossed did I become with the house plans that before I knew it early twilight of the short January day forced me to light the old kerosene lamp. I glanced outside and saw the horses crowding hungrily around the empty corral, waiting to be fed. I wished Louis would hurry home with the hay.

Suddenly I felt gay. In this raw land of rough wool, mukluks, and fur parkas, surely a man must sometimes long to see a woman in truly feminine garb. I would dress for Louis! Dashing to the corner trunk, I took out a gown from its wrappings of tissue paper. I filled a washtub with warmed snow water, poured in drops of Robe d'un Soir bath oil, and soaked in northern luxury. Emerging, I patted on pink talcum powder. Fragrances spoke louder than words. I hoped Louis' first whiff would put him on a sentimental, loving wavelength.

I slipped into the airy gown, and clouds of net billowed over my head and settled in swirls of misty layers. I peered into Louis' shaving mirror, but all I could see was the top of my head. Regretfully, I looked at the slender straps and rhinestone clips of my dancing pumps. Because the floor was cold and splintery, I would have to leave on my mukluks until the last minute.

I heard the hum of an engine. Louis! And it was only nine o'clock. I hurriedly tucked silk Peau de Boie roses in my hair. A loud knock. Why was Louis knocking? It must be to tease me, of course. I ran laughing to the door and flung it wide. Standing there, tall and somber in the feeble lamplight, was the serious, frightening, Royal Canadian Mounted Policeman who had dominated my last night's dreams.

Grim Reality

The Canadian Mounted Policeman at my door had the same eyes, the same features, the same grimness of the Mounty who had appeared in my dreams. I stood transfixed, staring. He, likewise, stood transfixed, staring. What did he think of this crazy woman, dressed in an airy gown in a crude, tiny, remote log cabin? I'll never know.

Fog billowed and writhed between us as the warm moist air of the cabin met the −50 degrees of cold. Was this Mounty real, or would he vanish, like the one in my dreams? A gust of wind whipped a snow-laden spruce, and powdery snow sifted over the shaggy fur of his buffalo coat. I realized suddenly that he was real. The filmy-net folds of my skirt gently swirled in the frigid air. Touching his hand lightly to his muskrat fur cap, he said, "My orders are to take you to the hospital. Your husband has been in a serious accident."

This then was what the dream had forecast. My tabby Annabel's frantic mewing as she rubbed her black fur against my legs brought me to reality. Far in the distance I seemed to hear someone else's voice answer, "Yes. I can be ready in a few moments."

I hastily fumbled into heavy wool slacks. With shaking hands I tried to tie on my sealskin mukluks with Annabel pouncing on the red pom-pon ties. What to do with her? What of poor Red, suspended from the barn rafters? Only this morning I had given him our last fork full of hay. I decided on a place for the cat: I lifted floorboards to the dugout cellar and dropped her there. She would be warm. There was dried fish enough in the cellar to keep her fed.

I slipped into my white fur parka, blew out the lamp, and closed the door. The patrol car sped toward the tiny log-cabin village of Mayo. Northern lights flickered, flamed, and writhed overhead. I clenched my hands, trying hard not to tremble. I didn't know whether it was from the intense cold, or the shock and worry over my husband. The constable drove without conversation. Did his manual tell him to say nothing when a human heart was breaking? Was this to be the end of the trail for Louis and me? Only three years a wife, but what a wondrous three years! Frontier life, love, happiness, and a way of living so different from anything I had ever experienced that every day was an adventure. But if Louis lived to be a cripple, what then? In this untamed land it took a strong, capable man to live the kind of life that Louis had chosen.

I was afraid to ask questions, afraid not to. Finally, I summoned courage and turned to the Mounty. "How long before he was found?"

"Six hours."

SIX HOURS! Six hours lying hurt at −54 degrees F.! Even if he lived, his hands and feet must be beyond saving. I swallowed hard. What would life mean to my beloved Louis if he could no longer climb the mountains after his beautiful white Dall rams? How would he saddle, bridle, and pack his horses? Would he ever walk again?

Gradually, gently, Constable Cruthers, for he had told me his name although it hadn't registered, told me what he knew. Louis, although he was still in shock, had related much. Later, I learned the full story:

Before leaving that morning, Louis had gone into the unfinished barn for a last check on the horses. There he had noticed a ragged, discarded eiderdown sleeping bag hanging on a nail. Vaguely wondering why I was so insistent on him taking a sleeping bag, he casually tossed it into the back of the truck. He was simply satisfying a whim of his wife. Although he had kept a heater under the truck for most of the night, the engine was still stiff. Nevertheless, he managed to start it. While waiting for it to get warm, he glanced at his watch. Six o'clock. He estimated he would reach Dawson City in about three hours. He eased the truck into low gear and the four big wheels on cold-stiffened tires lurched over our makeshift road. He reached the main highway in half an hour. A main highway in the Yukon in that year of 1956 was a narrow, winding, snow-covered road. A grader had recently plowed the loose snow. The road was slippery, but the truck rolled easily as it warmed to its work, and Louis made good time.

The headlights picked up two shiny eyes, and the owner, a silver fox, leaped gracefully across the road ahead. Near Stewart Crossing, a lynx stood for a frozen instant in the headlights, then quickly disappeared into the brush. The stars sparkled like points of chipped ice. Four miles past Stewart Crossing, Louis found a dead wolf. He stopped to look at it. The animal had probably been hit by a freight truck. The fur was winter-thick and beautiful. Louis dragged the wolf to the side of the road, intending to pick it up on his return.

Five miles farther he was surprised to see horse tracks. Although some of our horses were missing, he had no thought that they would stray this far. He stopped the truck and followed the tracks a few hundred yards. Hearing a nicker, he turned and saw Sally, one of our older mares, standing at the edge of a steep cliff. There were wolves about, and he knew she wouldn't be safe for long. The best he could do would be to pick her up with the truck on the morrow.

It was seven o'clock. He knew he must hurry if he was to reach Dawson and return home in one day. He put the truck to a steep hill. The wheels occasionally spun in loose snow. At the top of the grade the road turned sharply. Halfway around the turn, the truck skidded into the bank, rocked crazily, then bounded from the bank and shot straight across the road. It teetered for a moment on the edge, then plunged down an 80-foot bank. During the plunge it rolled over four or five times.

As the truck crashed down the precipitous slope, Louis thought that it sounded like a load of tin cans and iron barrels being dumped. The action was swift blur. Louis had no time to feel fright. The truck rolled over again, righted itself, then shot straight for a large spruce tree. It slammed into the tree, briefly coming to an abrupt stop. Both doors flew open. A 12-foot chunk of spruce sheered from the tree and flew across a nearby frozen lake.

The truck rolled again, and Louis was hurled out. Something hit his back, and suddenly, for the first time, he realized he might die. The truck stopped rolling, and Louis found himself suspended in the air, hanging from a steel angle iron on the bed of the truck. The sharp iron had pierced the front of his parka. He struggled for footing on part of the broken truck rack to lift himself free of the angle iron. He almost fainted from the sudden, excruciating pain in his left arm and left leg. He felt of the leg. His heavy wool tweed pants and thick wool underwear were torn away. His leg was wet with blood. Leaning over, he saw blood spurt from a huge wound from which the flesh had been gouged. The hole was almost large enough to hold both of his hands. Also, his left leg was twisted grotesquely at a right angle. It had to be broken. His cap was gone, and the bitter cold started to penetrate. He had to use his one good arm and one good leg to get off the truck or he would soon freeze to death.

He swung himself and caught a toehold on part of the rack. Slowly raising himself, he struggled to free his torn parka from the angle iron. His foot slipped, and in agony, he was again held suspended by the front of his parka, body swinging in the air. If he passed out from the pain he would be finished. He doubted if any cars would be on the road on this bitter cold day. It was also Sunday. Again he swung himself, caught another toehold, and with all his remaining strength pulled with his right arm, lifting his entire body until he was freed from the pinning angle iron. Then he slowly lowered himself to the ground. He crawled five or six feet from the truck so he could straighten his leg.

A golden orange tinged the horizon, and he knew it would soon be dawn. He thought of the barrel of gas on the truck. If he could find it, and somehow light a fire, he would have warmth. It would also be a signal for passing traffic. For a few moments it was a good idea. Then, he realized, a full barrel of gasoline would probably explode. He might burn to death. Some irony, he thought: he could burn to death out in the open at −55 degrees F.

Louis told himself, "Well, Brown, you've been in a lot of tough situations. You've managed to get out of all of them by yourself. This time, old boy, you're going to need help."

The icy yellow sun rose above the horizon. The first rays of dawn illuminated a nearby patch of snow, and there he saw the tattered sleeping bag he had tossed into the truck. Dolores' whim! It lay a mere five or six feet away. He couldn't reach it. Nor could he crawl to it. He grabbed one end of a splintered piece of the truck rack and tried to snag the sleeping bag. Again and again he stretched. Each time the end of the stick was inches from the bag. He turned on his side and made a last, desperate thrust. This time he managed to hook the bag and drag it to him. As best he could, he shook it free of snow. He spread it, and in agony crawled on, then pulled the rest over himself. Pain came with every movement. He thought of me, and murmured, "Dolores, I'm hurt and I'm hurt bad."

Brittle sunlight shone on the lake and Louis forced himself to wriggle his toes to keep them from freezing. He kept thinking that he must light a fire. He wondered if he was becoming delirious, for he heard a voice say, "Be still. Be still."

The hours drifted by. The voice constantly repeated "Be still." There was no way he could get out by himself. He was too badly injured. He wondered about his life. Had it been as good as it could have been? If he lived, could he do better? All his striving didn't seem to amount to anything at the moment.

Beside him a large red splotch spread in the snow. He was losing much blood. The bitter cold penetrated his body, and it was becoming nearly unbearable. He shivered violently, and he knew it was nature's way of working his muscles to produce body heat. He began to pray, "Oh God, give me strength to last. Help me to stand this cold."

He drifted into unconsciousness, and then revived. "God, I can't last much longer." He began to lose his vision. In the distance he heard an engine. It grew louder and louder, and hope rose. Then the engine noise faded. The vehicle had passed on by.

The mail truck, driven by Jimmy Close, was the only vehicle that traveled the road that day. Jimmy was making the run from Dawson City to Mayo. With him was one passenger, a priest, who was anxious to reach his destination.

As a small boy, Jimmy had often stayed with Louis in his trapper's cabin. Louis had always been proud of the boy's brilliance. The youngster had been full of imaginative pranks, and he was good company for the bachelor trapper.

Jimmy had rounded the sharp curve and noticed truck tracks that appeared to run over the bank. He slowed, intending to stop and look, but the Father was in a hurry. He had a mass to perform, and he wanted to be on time. He urged Jimmy to keep going. After all, only the mail truck would be traveling the road on such a cold day. Jimmy drove on, but the recollection of those tracks going over the edge of the road worried him. If someone *had* recently gone over in this terrible cold, he would desperately need help. Jimmy knew no other traffic was likely that day.

He stopped and slowly backed up. Louis heard the truck stop. He gathered his remaining strength in a desperate effort to save himself. He hollered with all the volume he could muster. Jimmy heard him. From the road he looked down the steep slope and called, "What are you doing down there?"

Louis recognized the voice of Jimmy Close. "Jimmy, I'm in a bad way." Louis couldn't see him, but he knew it when Jimmy stood over him. He felt Jimmy lift the eiderdown sleeping bag. When Jimmy saw the blood and broken bones he exclaimed, "Oh, my God!"

Jimmy and the priest ripped boards from the truck rack and carefully eased them under Louis to keep him straight. Then they put him onto a tarpaulin, and tied him in place. Both were small men, and Louis weighed 180 pounds. They couldn't carry him up the steep, icy, bank. Instead, they dragged him more than 100 yards down and across the nearby frozen lake to a swale in the road grade. Jimmy backed the truck to the spot. Then the two men carried Louis to the truck. With great difficulty, they lifted him into the back of the big diesel rig.

Jimmy instructed the priest, "You stay in the back with Louie and turn the propane heater on hot." But the priest was so rattled at Louis' terrible injuries, that he turned the control past the hot point and onto cold. Louis shivered violently all the way to the Mayo hospital.

Louis was aware of being carried into the hospital. He was placed on the floor of a hallway to await Doctor J. V. Clark. He heard Clark exclaim, "They're coming in here worse every day!"

"Doctor," Louis gasped. "I didn't try to build a fire. Something told me to lie still."

"Well, Louis, it saved your life. If you had moved around it would have kept the wound open and you would have bled to death. By lying still, you allowed the cold to check the flow of blood."

As he was rolled into the operating room, Louis called, "Please tell my wife that I'm hurt."

*   *   *

Constable Cruthers knew little of this as he rushed me to the hospital. He only knew that Louis was still in the operating room when he had left to find me. He knew too that Louis' injuries were serious. It was dark as the patrol car turned down the dimly lit street of Mayo. We moved slowly past the church, rows of log cabins. On through town, and down a winding dark road. The old two-storied frame hospital loomed under flaring northern lights. We drew up behind a large black station wagon that served as both ambulance and hearse. My heart stopped. Was I too late? Was Louis gone?

Demon Lights Dance

The hospital loomed in monstrous gloom as I faced the possibility that Louis might be dead. Trembling with fear, I climbed the creaking steps into a deathly silent, narrow hallway. I timidly pushed open a door. Vapors of ether almost took my breath. In a shadowed corner, a nurse stood solicitously over a narrow bed. Miss Evans, the matron, looked up, smiled, and beckoned. Squeaks rose from the rough wooden-planked floor at my every step. On the cot lay a man I didn't recognize. Could this gaunt, pale, haggard person possibly be the vigorous wind-tanned man I had kissed goodbye this morning? Louis' breath came in deep gulping gasps. He was alive! Tears coursed my cheeks. I turned to the nurse.

"His hands and feet?"

She smiled encouragingly. "He's a very lucky man to have been found in time. His hands and feet are all right. But his blood vessels were starting to collapse and it was difficult giving him blood plasma."

Louis, still unconscious from surgery, rolled his head from side to side. He whispered, "I can't last much longer. I can't. . . ."

"Oh, Louis dear." I bent and kissed him. My heart ached. What a terrible ordeal he had been through.

Miss Evans left to help another patient. Louis was in a men's ward, and I was conscious of curious eyes in sunken faces as other patients watched me. I sat on the edge of the bed and stroked Louis' bruised hand. I spoke words of encouragement, trying to pierce the veil of unconsciousness.

The matron returned and stood quietly, checking Louis' pulse. Then she spoke to me. "Dr. Clark is coming to check on your husband. It would be better if you returned early in the morning. Get a good night's rest," she urged. I knew she was gently telling me I would be in the way. Rest? When all that was dear to me was fighting for life?

I walked from the hospital into the dark and icy cold. Across the river in the Indian village dogs were howling mournfully. I stumbled in blind haste toward the town. I was so new to the North, and I lived in such a remote area, that I was a stranger in this tiny outpost of a town. Where would I go? Where would I stay?

I found the elegantly named, but rough, Chateau Mayo, the only hotel. No clerk appeared as I stood uncertainly at the reception desk. I didn't know the ways of the frontier yet. Later I learned that the custom was to take any vacant room, and pay in the morning. I left the hotel and paced the dimly lit streets, not knowing what to do. The log cabins of the town seemed to huddle in the terrible cold. Suddenly, I saw the North in all its terrible reality. Pervading all was the inhuman cold. Too, there was the desperate loneliness, unbearable hardships. The fabulous North? What irony! What a fool I was to have thought the North was a land of romance, of handsome Mounties, dashing dog teams. Did I think I was going to live on a snow-sparkling Christmas card, taking gay sleigh rides for the rest of my life?

In frozen uncertainty, I watched the translucent pink and green colors of the northern lights curl and billow across the black, diamond-studded sky. From the horizon rose a broad band of bright lavender. Quivering, it flashed and played among the stars. Suddenly a whip of white fire lashed across the heavens, then spread into a transparent veil, quivering as if blown by some gentle ethereal breeze. Faster it whirled, advanced, retreated, dazzling lights, eerie phantoms of the heavens. To me, in my terrible despair, it was a demoniac dance of death.

I turned and fled down the street. A loose malamute sprung from the darkness, snarling, and I kicked it aside in panic. I fled up a path to the door of a tiny low cabin that showed a dim light. I knocked. A silver-haired woman opened the door. She looked at me in surprise. "Why, come in child. What are you doing out on such a cold night?" I shook uncontrollably as I told her of Louis' accident, and explained that no one seemed to be at the hotel to rent me a room. She helped me off with my parka and made me sit by the warm stove. She hurried into the kitchen, calling back, "A spot of hot tea is what you need, my dear."

When she returned with the tea I stared in amazement. Her silver tea service was exquisite, with gentle curves, graceful scalloping, delicate detailing, with hand-chased decorations. I looked into the faded blue eyes that were shining with pride and love, and I understood. She bustled about pouring tea. The beauty of the tea set bestowed an elegance on her humble dwelling. I smiled as I remembered once placing my own ornate Winthrop pattern silver tea set on a stump as I served tea to my husband's band of Indian guides.

This lovely woman was Mrs. George Reynolds, who for many years was matron of the Mayo hospital, I learned, as I sipped the life-giving tea. "You needn't worry about your husband. I know him well. He's strong and healthy. The human body can take incredible abuse when it hasn't known dissipation. We are fortunate in having such a skilled doctor as Dr. Clark in our little frontier town."

It was true. I had heard that Dr. Clark was the best in the North. "He won't leave your husband's side as long as he is in danger. Be assured, Dr. Clark will give your Louis the very finest of care. Now don't worry."

That good and kind woman soothed my agitation. My teacup stopped shaking and I drank several cups of the stimulating hot liquid. "Louis will probably be in the hospital for several weeks. I'm alone most of the time. Why don't you stay with me?"

"Oh, thank you. It's good of you to offer. I don't really know what I'm going to do."

Mrs. Reynolds studied me intently and I nervously laughed. "I'm afraid your Yukon is too tough for me." Mrs. Reynolds smoothed her apron, smiled warmly, and commented, "My dear, people nowadays have silver spoons in their mouths compared with when I first came North."

"Yes. I suppose so." I wasn't convinced.

"Anyway," she continued, "you must stay the night with me. I've been lonesome for a good homey chat. You won't be able to go right to sleep, so don't fret. Let's visit."

I relaxed in the warm room, admiring eyes on the silver tea service, while I listened to the outpourings of a lonely heart. Suddenly, my hostess hurried from the room and returned with a package. Tenderly, she unwrapped a velvet jewel case and a small black book. She looked up and her eyes sparkled. "You know, I was a nurse with the Black and Tans in Ireland." A shock went through me. An Irish friend had once regaled me with bloody tales of the Black and Tans. Mrs. Reynolds snapped the lid of the black velvet case, and it sprung open, revealing a beribboned medal on red satin. She gently lifted the dull gold medal. Proudly she said, "King George the Fifth pinned this Medal of the Order of the British Empire on me for valorous service."

"What a great honor," I murmured, thinking how incredible it was that this woman who had once stood in Buckingham Palace to be

17

decorated by the King himself should now live on this remote frontier. Mrs. Reynolds handed me the little black book. "After the ceremony with the King, Queen Alexandra gave a tea party for all the nurses. She presented each nurse with this book. She was the most beautiful woman I have ever seen, but oh, what sad eyes. Her sister was the Czarina of Russia, and had been murdered."

"How in the world did you happen to come to the Yukon?" I asked. I was unaware that this wonderful lady was drawing me out of myself, freeing me, for a time, of worry over Louis. "My dear, life can take some very queer twists. By chance I learned of the dire need for a nurse in Mayo. At the time there was no doctor. There was only a nurse's station with no nurse, so I took the job." She threw both hands into the air. "What a time I had those first few years," she exclaimed, with a laugh.

"Were the Indians hard to nurse?"

"Not after I convinced them that they wouldn't die if I got rid of their lice!"

I was horrified, and said so.

"My dear, how could they live in the wilds and not have lice, without a single chemical bug killer to get rid of them?"

I remembered when Annabel had killed a squirrel, and got fleas from it. Soon both Louis and I were scratching. We had made a trip to town to buy flea powder.

Mrs. Reynolds continued, "Oh, we had some wild times. Once the hospital ran out of meat. That didn't stump Mrs. Erickson, our cook. She went out, shot a caribou, and carried the meat back to cook for the patients."

Mrs. Reynolds chuckled at my astonishment. "Usually things worked out all right, except for our pneumonia patients. We lost too many of them in those days."

"Was that the most dreaded disease?" I asked.

"Yes. It took the strictest kind of nursing. Our medicines were limited. You've seen the cemetery?"

I nodded.

"Most that lie there died of pneumonia."

She quickly rose as if to shake off the sadness of those days. "My goodness. It's two in the morning. I must put you to bed."

18

"I suppose so," I said, not really wanting to be by myself again after the cheerfulness of this woman. Just then the long wail of a husky drifted into the room. "They make me think something terrible is going to happen. That someone is going to die," I blurted, my mind flooding again with the scene of my poor husband as I had last seen him.

"Do you like music?" she asked.

"Very much. But not the jukebox kind," I laughed, half apologetically.

She went to the piano that stood in the corner. Her fingers ran nimbly over the keys, and I bolted upright. It seemed impossible. The crashing chords of Wagner's music drowned out the lonesome wail of the husky. Then a serene and lovely Mozart. She also played other melodies that I didn't recognize.

After a time, the music stopped. Mrs. Reynolds sat quietly at the piano, and I returned to my surroundings. She smiled, "Come. Let's go to bed. You'll want to go to Louis early."

She produced a voluminous flannel nightgown for me to wear, tucked me beneath a patchwork quilt, then kissed me on the cheek. How good it was to be mothered. I lay awake in the darkness and faced the possibility that Louis might be an invalid for the rest of his life. He might not even be able to earn our living. Even if in time he fully recovered, it would not be soon enough for him to take out big game hunters in the fall. That was our only dependable way of making a living.

I thought of the fifty-two dollars I had left at home. Most of that must be spent on necessities for Louis. What about doctor and hospital bills? How was I going to eat? I tossed and turned. Finally I got up and paced the cold board floor. I finally decided there was only one recourse: I would return to my old job in the Purchasing Division at the Washington State Capitol in Olympia.

It would be difficult telling Louis good-bye, but if I wasn't on the plane the next afternoon at three o'clock, weather could delay me for weeks. I must have been in shock. I wasn't thinking straight. I was used to making decisions, and this was a decision that seemed sound. I didn't think how Louis would feel, I didn't even think of poor Red, suspended from the barn rafters, or how the other horses were going to fare with no one to look after them.

To ease my worry, I pictured Louis happily sunning himself on the deck of a friend's yacht, and spending weekends at the Olympia hot springs. If there were medical complications, I could take him to

Switzerland where my brother Frank had recovered his health from a debilitating disease.

I wouldn't allow the North to separate us. I would send for Louis as soon as he could travel. Not a doubt crossed my mind—no hint that fate might have other plans for me.

The Wolf Pack

At dawn, after a short troubled sleep, I let myself out of Mrs. Reynolds' tiny log cabin. The temperature was 65 degrees below zero. Fog lay in the streets. Smoke from cabin chimneys rose straight into the air in stiff spikes. I hurried to the hospital and found Louis sleeping. I stood beside his bed, holding his hand. Through the old bubbly glass windows I watched a pale sun edge above the horizon.

Wilfred Gorden, one of Louis' old friends, arrived and stood beside me. We watched Louis' battered body rise and fall as he breathed in silence. I had difficulty holding in the tears. I was so alone now. I knew I must be strong for Louis, and I quickly wiped my eyes and blew my nose.

"I was at my wood camp six miles below your place," Wilfred told me, quietly. "Saw tracks of a pack of wolves headed your way."

Louis stirred, his eyes opened. He gave a faint smile, and feebly squeezed my hand. He had heard Wilfred.

Barely able to talk, he whispered, "Save the horses."

I knew what he meant. Our only hope of surviving financially was by our horses. We had to make the coming fall big game hunts. Thinking I must tell him of my plan to go back to my old job to earn money at once or lose my courage, I said, "Louis, I'm sorry, but I'm going to have to leave you."

"Yes. Go back home. Save the horses," he whispered.

He didn't understand.

"But Louis . . ." I started to say.

"Book a lot of hunters. I'll need every horse," he whispered.

"Louis, listen . . . ."

"Save Red."

Red? I had forgotten poor Red, helpless in his sling, with nothing to eat. The shock of Louis' near-death accident had distorted my thinking

Suddenly, I knew I could not leave our horses to starve to death. At that moment, I think, I became a Northerner. I suddenly realized what my duty was. I must carry on for my husband, and I must carry on for our horses. I couldn't abandon all our hopes and plans. My silly idea to head south and work to earn money made no sense.

I talked with Dr. Clark. "There's nothing you can do for Louis here," he assured me. "It will take time for him to heal, and he'll have to stay in the hospital."

Louis was in no shape to talk. He slipped in and out of an uneasy sleep as I sat near. Wilfred left, and in the quiet of the hospital ward, I made my plans, then quietly rose and left. I rushed into Mayo and arranged to buy three tons of hay for $500 on credit. Then I had a friend drive me the 20 miles home. As we drove up the snowy road, our 29 pack and saddle horses were huddled around the cabin. Icicles hung from their nostrils. The temperature was 72 degrees below zero. Never had I seen it so cold. Annabel scolded me for having left her locked in the cellar, but she was safe and warm and welcomed me with loud purrs and much rubbing of her fur on my legs.

After lighting a fire in the stove so the cabin would warm, I bundled up as I had never bundled before. "Take care of the horses," Louis had said. I determined to do my best. Icy claws snatched the warmth right out my body as I pitched hay to the poor, cold beasts. Poor Red, confined to his sling, was ravenous. The fire in the stove near him had gone out. I lit a fire in it with some difficulty. I put a tub full of snow on top of the stove to melt so Red could drink, then I put hay where he could reach it.

My routine became set. Twice a day I fed and counted the thin horses. Most wore long ragged hair, and there was no shine to their coats. Wolves frequently moaned nearby, day and night, and I just knew they were after our horses. Their howls and wails made the horses nervous. I could do nothing about it.

On the sixth morning after I had returned home, Donna, a little dun mare, was missing when I made the morning count at the corral. During the night the horses always trooped to a small wild meadow about a quarter of a mile from the cabin. There they pawed through the snow for grass. The meadow was sheltered by trees all around. I knew Louis would have gone there first to look for Donna, so I strapped on snowshoes and headed that way. I dreaded what I might find.

I found no sign of Donna in the first clearing, but as I snowshoed through a wide opening in the willows I found her. She stood with drooping head. I was puzzled to see that she had been walking in a tight circle, within her own tracks. Although she seemed dead tired, her ears were alert. I tried to lead her, but she wouldn't leave the trampled area.

Once, as I urged her to follow, I thought I saw a gray shadow slink furtively through the nearby brush. That alarmed me. Wolves were on my mind, and Donna's behavior only emphasized the thought.

Despite all my urging, Donna refused to move. Then I remembered that an old horseman had once told Louis and me how his father had doctored sick horses with rum. Was Donna sick? Or was she terrified of the wolves that had been howling near? Perhaps it was a bit of both. We had several gift bottles of over proof rum, left by our hunter-clients.

I shed my snowshoes and ran back over the packed horse trail to the cabin. I jerked the Hudson Bay point blanket off our bed and filled a thermos jug with hot water from atop the stove. I grabbed a box of Quaker oats, and stuck two bottles of rum inside my parka. As I ran back to Donna, my warm breath rose from beneath my face scarf to freeze on my eyelashes. I had to stop and hold the palm of my bare hand against my eyes to thaw the ice from my lashes. As I burst through a clump of willows, Donna was just bending her front legs to lie down.

"Noooo, Donna!" I screamed at her as I ran to her side. If she did lie down, I was sure I would never be able to get her up. I strapped on the blanket. I poured rum into a pail and diluted it with hot water. She drank greedily of this, but upset half. Then she ate some of the oats. She was so excited over the oats that she almost upset the pail again.

I then tried to lead her toward the cabin, but again she refused to move. She tried to lie down, and I slapped her in the rump as hard as I could. She lunged forward. Suddenly, from close by in the timber, came a low eerie wolf howl. Donna swiftly turned to face the sound. By this time my feet were becoming numb, and my hands ached. Terrified that both Donna and I would collapse, I took several gulps of rum myself, and poured the rest down Donna as best I could. Much of it spilled into the snow. I then broke off a big willow branch and whacked her away from her snow-packed haven and toward the cabin. Neither of us could walk straight. I later had to giggle at the meandering trail we left in the snow on that journey to the corral.

That night I hung kerosene lanterns at each end of the corral, and at intervals beat on a 45-gallon oil drum with horseshoes. I hoped this would keep the wolves away. Several days later three of our best pack horses, Jim, Suzy, and Maude, were missing at my morning count.

Taking my .270 rifle, I again went to the meadow. There I found the bloody remains of all three. As I walked up to one of the partly eaten horses, I came upon two gorged wolves, asleep in the snow. When I rammed a shell into the rifle chamber, the wolves heard the click. They leaped to their feet and ran for cover before I could shoot. The scene in that meadow still haunts me. Blood, hair, and horse parts were everywhere. It must have taken the entire pack to kill those three horses. Terrified, I fled home.

I was sick over the loss, and I worried that I wouldn't be able to save the others. I went to the meadow again, carrying the rifle, and there built two large fires, one on each end of the long meadow. I used plenty of kerosene to get the flames leaping high. I hoped the fires would frighten the wolves. Perhaps the horses could feed and get some rest. I knew from their behavior that the wolves had been harassing them. Day and night I frequently heard the blood-chilling howls and moans of wolves, both near and far.

The deep cold, the poor hay, and the constant harassment from wolves, took its toll. The poor horses were dangerously thin and weak. Each day, it seemed, they looked worse. One morning I went into the cellar and gathered every garden vegetable I had—mostly potatoes and carrots—and cooked them. As they cooled, I added what few oats I had left. I gave each horse a few bites, hoping it would help. I also strapped every blanket I could find on the animals. Perhaps the added warmth and extra food would keep them from going to the meadow.

One long exhausting day I tried to keep the horses home, patrolled for wolves with the rifle, packed water and food for Red, and tried to keep his stove going. I also tried to keep fires going in the meadow, retied blankets on horses, and kept the fire going in the cabin stove. The temperature hovered below the −70 degree mark. I finally collapsed on the bed and fell into a deep sleep.

When I awoke, the fire was out, and the cabin was cold. I had dreamed that Louis was dead. I was stiff, cold, still exhausted. I just knew there was no use in trying to save the horses. I had had no word from or about Louis for two weeks. He had remained critical for a time, and then his condition was upgraded to serious. But for my wonderful Indian neighbors across the Stewart River, I was basically alone, trapped with the horses. I didn't even dare drive to Mayo to see Louis in our one ton truck, for the road was choked with deep snowdrifts.

I checked my rifle, and stuffed shells for it in my pocket. No more horses were going to die in agony from the fangs of wolves. I could give them a far easier death. Could I really do it? I didn't know, but I headed for the corral with that terrible thought in mind. I was halfway there when Billy arrived. He wanted to borrow some .30-30 shells.

"What'ta matter?" he asked sharply.

Suddenly everything seemed terribly funny. I didn't realize it, but I was close to breaking. I babbled with hilarity how surprised the wolves would be when they found there were no more horses to kill.

Billy took my rifle, and ordered me into the cabin. He built a fire and made tea. I couldn't hold a cup, my hands were shaking so badly. Billy poured cup after cup of steaming tea down me. At last I began to get warm, and I broke down and sobbed the whole story of the wolf-killed horses, and of Louis' death.

Billy snorted. "How you know Louie die?"

"I dreamed it."

"Aiaa. Radio man he not say t'at," Billy scoffed.

Radio? Our batteries are frozen. "Billy do you listen to the radio every day?" I asked, hopefully.

"Sure. Louie great guy. He die, radio he say. He not say."

Billy returned home to get some wolf traps, and when he returned, Old Maggie, his wife, accompanied him. While Billy set out traps, Maggie, speaking brokenly, explained why Billy needed more .30-30 shells. Wolves had tried to kill their sled dogs. Billy had shot one big black wolf.

Billy and Old Maggie stayed long enough to see that I was warm, and that I ate some food, and had a good night's sleep. Billy cared for the horses for me for a day or so. It was heavenly to have them there, helping. But they had to return home, for Billy had traps out that had to be tended, and they had their dog team to care for.

Billy's wolf trapping wasn't very successful. In a few days, after he caught one wolf by the toes and it escaped, other members of the pack refused to go near a trap.

A few days after they left, after a long hard day of fighting the cold and caring for the horses, I sat half-drowsing beside the cabin stove. Suddenly, I heard a broken, heaving gasp from one of the horses near the barn. I knew the sound. A horse was fighting for breath. My God! Did a wolf have a horse down? Was he eating the poor creature alive? I opened the door, and icy air poured into the cabin. Then I heard the sound again. It came from the corral, where it was pitch black. I was so frightened that my knees shook, and I had to sit down.

What would Louis do? I knew he wouldn't sit down with shaking knees. I strapped on a revolver, fastened my parka, then, carrying Louis' hunting knife in one hand and a flashlight in the other, ran to the corral. Shakily, I climbed the pole rails, and inched my way around the corral, poking the flashlight ahead, peering into the darkness. The horrible gasps grew louder. In the dim light I saw a horse half lying on the ground, his head suspended.

"Tomtom," I screamed. His halter had caught on the post, and he was choking to death.

I leaped down and cut the rope. His head flopped to the ground. Tomtom didn't move. I was sure he was dead. Had the wolves chased him to force him into such a crazy predicament?

Wolves howled on a ridge behind the cabin, and I rushed into the cabin and came out with my rifle and fired several shots into the darkness. The howls stopped.

Next morning as I dressed I determined that I would be braver, more cheerful, and above all, I would use my head. In the terrible cold, I knew I could die with one slip of judgment. First, I decided, I would eat a good breakfast and try to add some fat to my 105 pounds. Perhaps I wouldn't feel the cold so much.

I fried a tall stack of hotcakes. They were delicious, with gobs of melting butter and hot maple syrup. As I polished them off, a shrill whinny sounded outside. Peeking through the door window was a horse. A slashed halter dangled rakishly from side of his head. Tomtom! I jumped from the table, laughing and sniffling. I ran out and hugged him around the neck. He was so gaunt and hungry—looking that it made me feel like a glutton, filling myself with hotcakes while he was starving. Dashing inside, I fried another stack of hotcakes and offered them to Tomtom. He devoured the entire stack in about two gulps.

I fried another stack, and carried them out to the poor, suspended Red. He hadn't seemed to be doing well. It seemed to me that his head drooped lower with each passing day. I gave him more hay than I did the others, and each day I melted a tub of snow water for him to drink.

As Red finished the last of his hotcakes, I heard Billy yell. I left Red and went out and waved. Billy beckoned me to the side of the cabin. He pointed to several depressions in the snow.

"What are they, Billy?" I asked.

"Wolf. Six'm. Him make'm last night. Him play around. Him lay down, rest."

My blood seemed to run cold. Were the wolves playing beside the cabin when I went to help Tomtom?

I made tea and Billy and I drank cup after cup. I served bread, and we smeared the pieces thickly with strawberry jam.

"Billy, does the owl lie sometimes?"

Billy glared. "How owl lie?"

"Well, you said Louis would die and now you say Louis not dead."

"Owl not say Louie die. He say white man die. White man die."

"White man die?"

Billy nodded. "Radio say silver mine white man shoot white man."

"Billy, I'm so glad your owl tells the truth."

Billy stood up to leave. "Your old man tough. Next winter run moose down on snowshoe. He all right soon."

I closed the door behind him, grabbed a towel, and sobbed in shame and relief. I was ashamed to remember when I first came North and married Louis that I had called Billy an ignorant savage. Was a human being a savage when he extended a hand of kindness and comfort to one who was in trouble?

A few hours after Billy left I felt terribly alone. I found a withered carrot and went out to check on Red. "Red, hey Red," I called, expecting to be greeted by the usual nicker. But there was no sound. I found his limp form hanging from the sling. There was no life in the body that had been my friend. I turned and ran. I wanted to flee this terrible place. It didn't matter where I went, just so it was away.

I ran past the cabin, the caches, the horses. I ran until I was exhausted, and then I plunged myself prone into a snowdrift. I was so tired, so cold, and so discouraged. Poor Red! I felt sorry for all of us. The unrelenting cold simply seemed too much. It was the cold that had nearly killed Louis. What was the use? The sooner the horses and I froze to death, the better. Why did Red have to die when I loved him so much?

Jack McLean's Valley

I lay in the snowdrift, numb with grief, exhausted, and cold. Was the whole world white? White snow, white sky, white trees. How long before I too would be frosty white? I was barely functioning because of exhaustion, fear, and worry over Louis. Something touched me. I shrank from it, and turned to see Copper standing over me. He was nudging me for sugar. His bony, long-haired frame little resembled the glossy, smooth Copper of summer. I realized that he too lived in a white world, fighting for survival along with all the other horses. And me. I too was fighting for survival.

Copper bent his head, nuzzling a pocket of my parka, and I threw an arm around his neck. Startled, the colt backed up, dragging me to my feet. I held on to him. He wasn't broken to ride, but he was gentle, a pet. With coaxing and petting, I leaned my exhausted body on him and guided him to the cabin door.

The stove was still warm, and I flung myself down on the bed and dropped into a sleep of exhaustion.

From the depths of oblivion I heard a knock. A wavering voice drifted into my dreams. "Mrs. Brown, are you home? The R.C.M.P. is here."

I shivered awake. The cabin was bitterly cold. Annabel tumbled from my chest as I struggled to my feet. The police! Had Louis died? Fearfully, I opened the door.

It was Constable Cruthers, who had driven me to Louis' side on the day of the accident. Briskly, he said, "Mrs. Brown, I need some information about the accident before I can file my report."

At that moment Billy came around the corner of the cabin carrying a huge armload of firewood. After building a fire, he stood solemnly by the stove while I answered questions about the demolished truck. When Cruthers rose to leave, Billy stepped forward and faced me, "You go with policeman. See Louis. Billy take good care horses. You go."

"But Billy, it's a long way for you to come every day to feed the horses," I objected weakly.

But he was determined. "Louie damn sick. Miss white squaw like hell. You go." I hesitated, but only momentarily. I did desperately long to see Louis. Maybe if I saw him, I could return to caring for the horses with more courage.

The ride to Mayo was interminable. I hadn't seen Louis for several weeks. Was he gaining? Were his bones healing? Had there been complications? I wanted to urge the Constable to drive faster. At last I ran up the hospital steps. I almost collided with Miss Evans, the matron, bustling down the hall, balancing a tray. She smiled, "Oh, Mrs. Brown, you won't be able to see your husband for about an hour. Dr. Clark is examining him right now."

Trying to hide my disappointment, I left word for Louis that I would return soon. I caught a ride into town with the hospital's janitor, who left me at Mrs. Reynolds' cabin.

That dear soul threw her arms around me. "How glad I am to see you. I've worried so much about you being out there all by yourself. My dear, you look healthy, but oh, you are so thin!"

She turned to her husband, who I had not met. "George, this lady is an American, like yourself."

"What state are you from?" I asked.

"Kentucky."

"Oh, you're from the state of fast horses."

"Yep, and fast women too." George's eyes twinkled mischievously as he chuckled at my shocked silence.

After a brief visit and a promise to return for dinner, I went back to the hospital. I opened the door to the men's ward, and was almost bowled over by a blast of noise. The high, old-fashioned bubbly windows rattled to the blare of *Oklahoma*, played by a stuttery old phonograph. Gordon McRae was bursting his lungs singing something about the cows in the meadow. But from the vibrating floor, I thought the herd was stampeding through the ward. Indian children shrieked as they dashed under, over, and behind beds, playing hide-and-go-seek. Two huskies raced after them. Clenching my teeth, I headed for the phonograph. On my way, I passed old Scotty, who was in the hospital for treatment of a weak heart. I wondered if this would bring on a fatal heart attack. However, the doughty little Scotsman winked as I passed. He was tapping his foot against the foot of his bed in time with the music.

30

I shut the phonograph off, and headed for Louis. He smiled happily at me. "G..g..g..good to s..s..see y..you," he stuttered. Startled, I wondered if his injuries had impaired his speech. I looked closely, and was astonished to see his teeth chatter. Puzzled, I removed my parka and spread it over him. Then I felt the icy coldness of the room.

Scotty yelled, "Noth'n to worry about, Mrs. Brown. That damned fool janitor was in such a rush to get to town that he forgot to stoke the furnace. When he comes back, if he ever does, he'll jam it so full of wood he'll have us sweat'n!"

I don't know if it was from the excitement of seeing me, or a reaction to a recent medical treatment, but Louis suddenly became violently ill. I lifted him in my arms and put a cold cloth on his head. About then Dr. Clark arrived, brows coated with frost. One glance at Louis, and he shed his parka and mittens and went to work on him. In a little while Louis felt better, and the room slowly began to warm.

Louis wanted to know all about the horses. I reluctantly told him that wolves had killed Jim, Suzy, and Maude. He shook his head sorrowfully, and I hastened to tell him that all the others were doing fine. I didn't have the courage to tell him that Red was also dead. As I looked at the massive casts on Louis' leg and arm, I despaired. How could he ever guide hunters in the fall? If he couldn't, where was the money going to come from to pay his medical bills?

Once during that visit, Louis plucked at my sleeve and whispered brokenly, "Sheep hunting's over for me."

I buried my face in his neck. I loved him so much. "Louis, you'll be taking hunters to sheep for years and years to come," I said, encouragingly. I feared he was right, but I wasn't going to admit it, and I certainly didn't want him to believe it. We silently clung to each other.

I heard an object drop on the floor nearby. I noticed for the first time that the bed across the way was occupied by an old silver-haired man. He had dropped his pipe. He was fumbling over the contents of a side table with gnarled, heavily veined hands. Louis saw me looking at him. "That's Old Jack McLean. He's blind. Go help him."

I picked up Jack's pipe and placed it in his trembling hand. He turned his sightless eyes toward me. "Who are you?"

"Louis Brown's wife."

"Well, I'm glad to meet you. I know your husband well."

"Louis has often said you're the best prospector in the North, Mr. McLean," I said, truthfully.

The old man beamed broadly as he happily lit his pipe. He called over to Louis, "Louis, when spring comes, we'll be roaming the silent valleys the same as always. We'll catch fish and shoot moose. Better not tackle hunting that Bonnet Plume River country the first year after your smashup. That river can be deep and treacherous after a good rain. Take me along, Louie, and I'll show you my ol' valley near Castle Mountains. We could give your dudes the damndest hunt they ever had."

Louis' face lit up. "Jack, I'd almost forgotten about that place."

"Well, I ain't," Jack said, puffing his pipe. He jabbed the pipe at the ceiling, "The big rams stay on them grassy shelves high up on the west side of the valley. Now, on the other side there's a pass that's overrun with arctic marmots. That's where the grizzlies hang out. Once I even seen six thousand caribou up the northern part of the valley."

"No moose?" I asked, casually. I wasn't really interested in that valley. Too many problems occupied my mind, but I wanted to be polite to the old man.

Jack snorted, "Jist watch you don't get gored by them monsters. I've seen them there with seventy-two-inch spreads a-plenty."

As the old man talked, his face glowed. He was no longer weighted by illness, blindness, tragedy, or old age. We were in his beautiful valley, surrounded by snowy peaks. The valley floor was a carpet of caribou moose. In the heart of the valley was a deep blue lake chuck full of speckled trout. Wild ducks rippled the silvery surface.

Jack chuckled. "Forgot to mention. Ptarmigan flying all over the place. Used to make me mad. Always seem like they was makin' fun of me. Laugh'n in their birdlike way. Now, when loons laugh, it's sort of eerie and scary. But them damn ptarmigan laughed like they'd played a joke on me. Made me feel like a fool."

Jack's voice grew weak. "It's the only place in the North that has so much game in such little space. Louie, you'd better hunt there this year."

Louis humored the old prospector. "Sure, Jack. Sounds great."

"And," Jack added, "it's only three days fast walk'n from Keno."

I returned to my husband's bed. "Louis, do you know the place Jack is talking about?" I asked. Louis nodded. "Some time I'll show you on the map." Jack called me back to his bedside. "I've tramped over most of the North, but my valley—at least I call it my valley—is the best."

I sensed the loneliness of the old fellow. I felt the homesickness he felt for the valley he loved. I sat beside him and as he talked he was again a young man, roaming free. He breathed the winey spruce-filled air of the high country, and he thrilled to the sight of his first Dall ram. He remembered the deep grunt of a moose, and lived again the thrill of having a silver-tipped grizzly in his gun's sights.

I returned to Louis. There were tears of understanding in his eyes. I turned quickly to hide my stinging eyes, but Jack had forgotten us and had gently dropped off to sleep. Louis whispered, "Blind, and one of his legs will be amputated soon. He'll never see his valley again. Old prospectors like Jack never know when it's time to die. They're a wonderful breed."

The pipes began knocking and banging. Scotty snorted, "Thank God that damn janitor is back."

Visiting hours over, I kissed Louis, promising to return later in the day. I ran most of the way back to town. Indian families were moving from their village on the far side of the Stuart River to the outskirts of Mayo. Unable to feed their sled dogs, they had turned them loose to roam and feed among the white man's garbage cans. I feared the vicious animals.

I picked up our mail at the post office and had to dodge a dog fight as I left. I was surprised to find several letters from hunters. Opening one from Michigan, I gasped when a check for $300 dropped out. *Three hundred dollars!* It was a deposit for a hunt. A fortune. It would pay many of our debts. But what if Louis couldn't hunt? An idea leaped into my head, but it so terrified me that I quickly put it out of my mind.

Mrs. Reynolds served me a delicious chicken dinner, with hot cornbread and homemade blueberry pie. How good it was to visit with this genteel, but determined, English woman.

When I rose to return to the hospital, Mrs. Reynolds hurriedly pulled a wool shawl over her head and stepped outside to look at her thermometer. "My dear, it's 77 below. You must cover your face." She dug out a long white scarf and tied it over my nose and mouth.

It was dark, and the northern lights rippled green and pink chiffon streamers. On this night the mystery of those many-hued lights thrilled me. I was full of joy. With Louis' survival certain, I again felt the enchantment of the North.

Louis was eagerly waiting, but he scolded, "Dolores, don't come when it's this cold. You'll get frostbite."

"What! An old Yukoner like me staying away because of the cold? Besides, I don't lie out in the cold for six hours like someone I know," I teased.

Louis smiled at my poor joke.

I hated to leave, but both of us knew I had to return home to our horses. Much depended on them. To console us, I told Louis that Dr. Clark had said he could go home in April. "I'll get everything ready for you. Oh, it'll be wonderful having you home."

"Honey, don't go to a lot of extra work for me. I'd be happy with just a big spruce tree to sleep under."

As I left, I said goodbye to Jack. "So you think your valley would be an easy hunt?"

"Hell yes. I know every inch of it." He lowered his voice, "You tell Louie he can hunt in my valley, and I'll help him."

"Could you show me where it is?"

"Course. I can pinpoint it so you could get there blindfolded." I cringed, but the irony of his remark escaped him.

"I'll bring a map next time I come, Jack."

"Yep. A big one, and I'll explain to you the exact spot where you can get a beller'n moose, or a grizzly that has an eye on your hide!"

I laughed. "I'd love that. Maybe I'll see your valley some time."

"Take you there myself, just as soon as I shake this bed," Jack smiled. He puffed on his pipe and blew a smoke ring. It slowly widened, enclosing us in an impossible dream.

The Great Furniture Haul

I returned to the ranch. Immediately I rushed to the corrals and counted horses. All there. If possible, they looked thinner, but none had been lost. Billy had done a good job caring for them in my two-day absence. The break from the responsibility, and seeing Louis, had helped. I felt much better.

As I stood looking at the horses, a dazzling shaft of light shot across the land to pierce the pale opal clouds with golden shafts of fire. The sun! Oh, the sun! Its first time above the horizon since November! Three months without direct view of that wonderful golden star. Those who have not survived a long dark Northern winter cannot possibly understand the joy of seeing the long-absent sun when it returns. Like the ancients, I wanted to build a huge fire to welcome it back. I wanted to dance in wild abandon. I wanted to help destroy the enemies of the sun—chase back the north wind, break up the ice, melt the snow. I laughed with joy.

I dashed into the cabin and stopped in wonder. A miracle! The log walls glowed like molten amber. Sunshine! How beautiful. I ran outside again, wild with ecstasy. The horses too sought out each tiny patch of sunshine. What a glorious world!

Next morning I leaped from bed and ran to the window. The sky was cloudless. The sun was free. How much higher would it climb today? Each day now it gained several minutes in its battle against darkness.

Bubbling with happiness, I decided to start readying at once for Louis' homecoming, although that event was several months away. The log walls must be washed, the floors scrubbed, and a few pieces of furniture hauled from the cache across the river where most of my things were stored. Originally, they had come from my apartment in Olympia, Washington. I wondered if I could talk Billy into hauling the furniture over with his dog team. I realized it would be hazardous, since the pieces I wanted were large and the trail was steep.

By noon it was actually warm—only twenty degrees below zero. I moved everything out of the cabin except bed, stove, and table. With the broom I attacked the detested rough plank floor. It was always dusty, and the splinters tore my satin mules. The bed was too heavy to move, so I crawled under it, and was vigorously sweeping out a corner when I heard CLUMP, CLUMP, CLUMP. Hastily, I backed out from under the bed and sat in shock.

"Copper, get out! This is no barn!" I yelled at the inquisitive colt. Copper, looking smug and self-satisfied, arched his neck around the stovepipe and helped himself to a slice of toast. A horse in the house! Ridiculous! The clumsy colt looked so funny, I burst out laughing. My merriment turned to concern as Copper stood looking over dishes and pans of food on the table. He was hungry. How was I ever going to get him out before he wrecked the place?

I snatched at his mane because he didn't have a halter, and tried to turn him. He sidled into the stove. Maybe I could back him up. "Back, Copper, back," I urged, pulling and then pushing.

But his rear wouldn't steer, and the washstand crashed to the floor. Frightened, Copper reared, and his head cracked against a ceiling beam. I dived back under the bed to avoid his flailing hoofs. I heard a shattering smash as dishes hit the floor, and I peeked out in time to see Copper departing through the door with the tablecloth between his teeth.

The log walls were grimy with spruce smoke and moose grease—a result of frying steaks. I was busily scrubbing them with plenty of soapsuds when Billy knocked. I yelled, "Come in."

Billy gave a puzzled look at the almost empty room. "Move Mayo?"

"Oh, Billy, no. I'm cleaning. What on earth are you carrying?"

He grinned. "Fish. Hungry, you?"

He carried a huge, freshly caught, lake trout.

"Billy, it's as big as a log. You catch'm?" I tended to revert to his abbreviated English when conversing with him. This says something about our relationship, I suppose. He certainly didn't adopt my style of English.

"Sure, catch'm me. Your old man catch'm little fish. Billy catch'm big." The old Indian's eyes twinkled as he teased.

"Billy, carry it out to the scales. I'm dying to know how much it weighs."

We waited for the scales to balance. Bending close, I exclaimed, "Sixty-four pounds! It's a monster."

Billy chuckled.

"Did you really bring this for me?" I asked.

"Sure."

"How did you know I was back?"

Billy snorted, as if I should have known the answer. "Owl, he tell me."

I sighed. "I wish owls would talk to me."

Billy gave me a keen glance. "Owl he talk to white squaw. No savvy owl talk, you."

"But Billy, I try hard to understand. But to me the owl just says WHOOO WHOO."

Just then a horned owl flew overhead and landed on a nearby spruce. He began to talk. "Billy," I whispered, "What does he say?"

A mischievous grin quivered on Billy's face. "He say, white squaw give Billy magazines. Good pictures."

I laughed. "Of course. Come in. I'll give you a whole stack."

Billy couldn't read or write, but he spent hours looking at the pictures of *Life* magazine. I had found one picture that I was anxious to show my Indian friend, and I wondered what his reaction would be.

I handed him a famous photo of a well-known Indian. Billy looked long at the picture, then he chuckled. "Me."

Billy was right. Every detail matched—eyes, nose, chin, solemn expression. The photo was an almost-replica of the Indian who sat facing me.

'Yes, Billy. You do look like Sitting Bull, one-time great chief of the Sioux."

"Chief. Once, me," he said.

"Yes, I heard you were chief of the Mayo Indians. But you gave it up. Why?"

Billy grunted in disgust. "Indian no fish, Indian no hunt. I no want to be chief to lazy Indian."

It was true that Billy had tried to get his people to fish and hunt in the old way. However, white man's shoot-'em-up movies and bottled beer were greater attractions. Billy resigned in defeat, and moved into the woods near our ranch.

I nervously cleared my throat. "Billy, I want to talk big business with you."

Billy looked at me perplexed. I explained, "I mean big powwow."

Billy nodded his understanding. "Sure. Big powwow." Then he chuckled. "Long time ago had big powwow. Dance six days, six night times. Beat eight drums. EIGHT DRUMS! he repeated, trying to impress me with the importance of that long-ago occasion.

"Well, Billy," I said, lamely, "I'm afraid there won't be any drums at this powwow. Maybe instead we can have a cup of tea."

Usually, Billy stirred several teaspoons of sugar into his tea, and drank it in one gulp, then asked for more. On this day he drank his tea slowly, and refused a second cup. Not until he had gone did I discover that I had absentmindedly filled the sugar bowl with flour.

Without a change of expression, Billy finished drinking the gluey mess, too polite to tell me. Then he said, "OK. powwow."

"Billy how are your dogs?"

"Dogs, him good."

"Is your toboggan strong?"

"Toboggan, he strong."

"You know that big old cache of ours across the river, not far from your cabin."

"I know."

"Would you move some furniture from the cache to this cabin with your dog team?"

Billy slowly turned and looked out through the door window at the stack of furniture outside. Hurriedly, I explained. "Louis needs a large chair to sit in. He has a big cast on his leg and arm."

Billy nodded. "OK. When you want?"

"Why, tomorrow, or next day, I guess."

"Tomorrow go to town. Next day."

"Fine. Will you mail a letter for me?" I asked.

"OK. See you in morning." And Billy left with his magazines.

The stars still glittered brightly and only a faint mist of white and gold showed the approach of dawn when I heard Billy and his dog team coming down the trail. I handed him the letter, and watched him hang grimly to the toboggan as it skidded around a bend in the trail, then disappeared in a flurry of snow.

No sooner was Billy gone than I felt a sense of apprehension. What had I done? I had accepted the $300 deposit check and sent Mr. Meade Ion, of Gross Point, Michigan, a receipt reserving him a 20-day hunt starting August 10. Surely, Louis wouldn't recover in time to take that hunt. How would we provide the hunt?

Suddenly overwhelmed by a feeling of panic, I wanted to dash after Billy and get the letter back.

I was surprised when a worried Billy arrived at the cabin early the next morning.

"Billy, what's wrong?"

Angrily, he said, "Store guy no good. Buy big box grub, me. No say want pickles, me. No say want cake, me."

I went out and looked at the large box of groceries in his toboggan. Included were many items that Billy would never think of eating. Then I saw a large scrawled name on the box. "Why, Billy, you picked up the wrong box of groceries. This belongs to old Mrs. Marshall."

Billy stood aghast. I told him, "Take it back home and eat it up. Next time you go to town you can buy Mrs. Marshall another box of groceries."

Billy looked at me as if he hadn't heard right. He exploded. "Billy steal? NO."

"Listen. It's 45 below zero. You can't make that long trip back to town now." It was five miles from Billy's cabin to the highway, and another 20 miles to Mayo.

Without a word, Billy straightened his dog team and headed for Mayo.

I waited two days, giving Billy time to rest from his two long trips to town. I then snowshoed up the trail. Reaching the river, I was careful to follow the upright sticks Billy used to mark the trail. I was crossing the mighty Stuart River, where treacherous air holes could appear. I remembered how Ed Kimball and Freddy Harper had driven on the ice up the Stuart in Ed's old White truck to get a load of hay. They made the trip up without difficulty. On the return they saw fog ahead. Freddy told Kimball, "Better look first."

Kimball, always in a hurry, said, "Oh, that's all right. We came this way six hours ago." Then he stepped on the gas.

When they reached the fog the truck plunged into the river and the two found themselves in nine feet of water, looking up at the hole in the ice. They managed to swim out, but it was 44 degrees below zero, and they were four miles from town. They struggled along the riverbank until they were near a sawmill close to town. They tried to climb the bank, but Kimball fell down and couldn't get up because his clothing was frozen and stiff. Freddy managed to climb the bank and get help.

Both men carried lifetime reminders that they should have checked the ice before driving over it—even though they had passed only six hours earlier. Kimball froze toes, Freddy his ears.

I breathed a sigh of relief when I had crossed. Then I took to the steep trail up the bench overlooking the river. Billy and Maggie lived on this high, flat table-land, and I followed Billy's well-packed trail. Rounding a sharp bend I almost jumped out of my mukluks. A large black wolf lay on the trail ahead. Hearing a chuckle, I looked up and saw Billy watching me.

"Billy, you shot him?" I managed to ask.

He nodded. "Night time. Almost kill dog."

"Can you move my furniture today?"

"Sure. Come. Maggie make tea. By 'n by haul furniture."

As a special treat, we ate smoked fish with our tea. When there was no more tea to drink, Billy hitched up his dog team. Maggie and I trailed behind, and Maggie talked all the way in the Indian dialect, which I don't understand. Billy didn't bother to reply.

The cache was chuck full from floor to ceiling. Billy looked at it with apprehension. An owl sat in a spruce tree nearby and hooted loudly. I wished it would shut up for fear that it was telling Billy not to move my furniture.

Billy asked, "What you want?"

His eyes almost popped out when I pointed to a large phonograph and radio combination. The fact that we had no electricity didn't matter to me. I was starved for music. Just knowing this machine was capable of making glorious music would help. I hoped that somehow Louis could weld a handle on it so I could turn the record and get sound from it.

Without a word, Billy staggered out with the bulky piece and fit it between the handlebars in the rear of the toboggan.

Not once had Maggie stopped talking. As Billy yanked up the sled brake and started to leave, I yelled, "The chair," and Maggie shrieked.

Billy stopped, disgruntled, and returned. Over and again I explained the importance of having that large red leather wing chair for Louis. We tried to wedge it in front of the phonograph, but it hung over the wheel dog. We tried fitting it edgeways, sideways, upside down. It was impossible. Finally, I had the bright idea of putting a trunk in front, and tying the chair on top of the entire load. This worked.

Billy carefully roped everything tightly to the toboggan. The dogs pulled the load to the edge of the bench, where Billy stopped them. Billy and I stood looking down the steep trail, while Maggie's tongue clacked on. I then looked at my precious load of furniture. Its value, I estimated, was about $2,000.

Billy shook his head and began unsnapping his dogs from the toboggan. "Toboggan go fast. Run over dog."

There was a sharp curve halfway to the bottom of the bench, with three large spruce trees at the edge of the trail. I didn't know how we were going to handle this, but Billy had a plan.

Maggie took charge of the dogs. Billy would run beside the toboggan and steer it clear of the trees. After I pushed the load over the edge, I was to be the brake.

Billy yelled, I pushed, Maggie screeched, and the dogs howled. Gathering momentum, the toboggan leaped forward. Down the steep icy trail it streaked. Billy futilely tried to keep up. We hit a dip, and the toboggan spurted ahead in a blur while I desperately hung on. The toboggan gave another lurch. Billy tripped and spun like a top, and the toboggan and I left him behind. My feet shot out from under me, but I grimly hung on. I was dragged at increasing speed and I felt like I had hold of a bolt of lightning.

Trees shot toward me. I tried to steer the runaway, and managed to make it veer slightly. The sled grazed the trees as we flashed by. I fell, rolling in the snow, as the toboggan slid across the river ice. Billy and I sat in the snow, stunned, staring at each other. Maggie stood pumping her arms up and down, howling with mirth.

Billy got up, brushing snow off. "Your old man damn mad. Billy bust'm chair."

"Well, we didn't really break it, Billy," I said. Then I added, "When we haul the next load . . . ."

"No." Billy said with great certainty. "No more haul furniture."

He hitched the dogs and drove at a sedate pace to our cabin. There, with great relief, he unhitched the dogs, and unloaded the sled.

Happy days followed while I prepared for Louis' homecoming. I worried, though. How was I going to look after an invalid when we had no running water, no bathroom, and no corner drugstore?

Louis Comes Home

May. Breakup. It came with a deep booming crash as great chunks of ice slammed together and were swept down the river. Thousands of sandhill cranes beat the northern skies with tireless wings, their rusty-hinge voices drifting far ahead of the straggling flocks. Geese in orderly Vs flew over the awakening land. The horses basked dreamily in the warm sunshine. All this was wonderful, but, for me, best of all, Louis came home.

Leaning heavily on his crutches, Louis breathed deeply of the tangy moist fragrance of the surrounding forest. Longingly, he looked down the trail, but he was too weak to venture beyond the doorstep. We stood listening to the sounds of wilderness. A baby raven on a fence rail squawked loudly to be fed. From the wild meadow came the call of a sharptail grouse. Nearer, sounded the bark of a hunting fox.

Louis counted horses. Smiling, he turned to me, "Eleven. That's enough for a two-man hunt. The Yukon hasn't licked us yet."

"No, but it came close," I said, leaning my head on his broad, but still bony, shoulder.

Louis could only remain up for a short time. I helped him into warm flannel pajamas. I was shocked at his thinness, his protruding ribs and backbone. He still suffered from the effects of the blow he received on the back from a chunk of spruce tree. I spent hours massaging the area, trying to promote healing. I wouldn't allow him to know the concern I felt. Hunting season was a little over three months away, and I wondered how such an emaciated and weak man could even think of guiding a hunt.

Next morning I was awakened by Louis' kiss. "Wake up. We have company." My eyes flew open. "Who?"

"Shhh," Louis cautioned. "Look up between the ceiling logs." I raised my eyes, and there among the rough overhead beams I saw two beady black eyes staring down at us. It was an ermine, still in winter white, with a black-tipped tail. It squeaked and flicked back through a hole under the eaves.

Louis was sitting in the big red-winged chair when Billy arrived to visit. With sharp, humorous eyes, he took in the cumbersome casts and chuckled, "He sure big man. Take big chair."

"Billy, I told Louis how hard you worked to bring it."

Louis grabbed the Indian's hand. "Thank you for looking after Dolores."

Billy snorted. "White squaw tough. Look after self." Then he handed me a package. Inside were a pair of pants I had recently purchased for Billy.

"Didn't you like them, Billy?" I asked.

He scowled. "No good."

"But Billy, these are cowboy jeans."

"What's matter cowboy? No meat on leg? Got meat on leg, me. Tell store man cowboy pants too skinny."

The old Indian was so serious that Louis and I didn't dare laugh until he had gone.

Billy had brought disturbing news. When the river ice had jammed at the bend near our ranch, two of our horses, Old Dan and Baldy, had crossed to the far side. It was too dangerous to bring them back on the now-rotten ice. How were we ever going to bring them back home? Billy left, saying he would keep an eye on them.

Louis refused to be babied. Against my wishes, he made his trips outside when necessary. The first time he laughed at my anxiety. When he returned, he teased, "It's the outhouse that made the Viking tough."

The river boomed, crashed, and rumbled as floating ice smashed into an ice jam at the bend. Louis and I stood on the bank watching, awed by the gigantic forces at play. Huge blocks of glacier-blue ice rose 10 and 20 feet into the air as they rolled in a massive jumble. Relentlessly, the river brought more ice to batter the jam. Water rose, and candle ice near shore tinkled as it shattered. Now the great mass moved, grinding, shaking the ground. Finally the immense ice dam gave way, and the water swiftly subsided, as the river swiftly floated the jumble downstream.

The conquering sun grew warmer, and day after day Louis lay under its vitalizing rays. We thrilled at the sight of thousands of sandhill cranes circling high, the rush of their wings whispering in the wind. Too, there was the lovely sight of graceful white swans glistening in the warm rays of the sun as their broad wings pushed them across the deep blue sky. If winter is the silence of expectancy, spring is a stupendous ovation to pulsing, precious life.

Gradually, Louis' hospital pallor was replaced by a healthy tan. With increasing strength came restlessness. Louis wanted to be out and around, but the crutches limited him. Then one day he told me he was hungry for fish. He got out his old shovel-nosed poling boat. Nervously, I pumped up an old tire tube for a lifesaver, and tied a heavy bow line on the boat.

If Louis, with his heavy arm and leg casts, fell overboard, I just knew he would sink like an anchor. But he refused to wear the tube, and I could only sit in the bow, ready to toss it over his head. Our 10-horsepower outboard motor pushed us down the Stuart River. We headed for a five-mile-distant Indian fish camp at the mouth of a horseshoe-shaped slough. There, Louis knew, whitefish migrate into the slough for summer feeding.

The swift current and the humming motor rapidly carried us downstream. Louis' face was radiant, and his eyes flashed with excitement. Free at last! The hospital was behind him, and he needed no crutches to maneuver the boat.

As we neared the fish camp, the current became swifter, and sweepers—trees fallen into the river from the bank—threatened us. Nervously, I fingered the rope I had tied to the boat, wondering how I would pull my husband from this swift water if I had to. I was relieved to see the old tent poles and rude drying shed of the deserted Indian camp. Louis nosed the boat toward the mouth of the slough. Then he exploded, "Damn!"

A large tree had fallen across the narrow opening, blocking entrance to the slough. It lay just beneath the surface. Louis edged the boat close and studied the log. "Well, it has no knots, and it's slick!" he muttered. He turned the boat away from the log and headed toward shore. "There used to be another channel on the other side of this sandspit. I'll let you out. You go see if a boat can get through," Louis suggested, guiding the boat to shore.

I jumped out and stood looking at an impossibly narrow channel, when I heard the revved-up motor. Spinning around, I saw Louis circle into the river, then point the boat at the partly submerged log. The boat shot ahead. Louis was going to try to slide the boat over the log. He had tricked me to get me out of the boat.

I fluttered and squawked like an old mother hen. Despite my frantic signals to stop, Louis sped past, headed for the log blocking the slough. The engine roared, then stopped as Louis jerked it from the water as the bow of the boat shot over the log. He sat with a triumphant grin as the length of the boat slid up and over the log. The boat plopped back into the water on the slough side. Louis restarted the outboard and came to the beach to pick me up. My knees shook, my heart pounded, and I had an overwhelming desire to push him overboard.

Instead, I climbed aboard and slammed the tire tube over his head. Louis laughed with glee, and I realized it was the first hearty laugh I had heard from him since his accident. He had suffered so much, and now he was experiencing a wonderful release. Although I was a nervous wreck, I shut my mouth.

Louis rigged his fishing tackle with a tiny spinner, and soon he was catching plump whitefish. After we had enough for a feed, we started a fire on the beach. While waiting for the fire to burn down to cooking coals, I dug some thick yellow bear roots. Louis fried the fish while I sliced bear root into another skillet. We were hungry, and enjoyed the delicately flavored white-fleshed fish, and the parsnip-flavored roots.

As we ate, Louis pointed to a clearing, being overgrown by young poplar trees. "The old stage road from Mayo to Whitehorse ran through there. One spring, years ago, Ed Burnell, a retired mounted policeman, was walking down the old stage road in almost that exact spot when a grizzly charged him from behind and knocked him flat, and then mauled him. He was slightly deaf, and probably didn't hear the bear coming. Ed managed to hang onto his rifle. His dog fought off the bear, giving him a chance to load the rifle and shoot. He killed the bear with one shot."

We ate in silence for a while. I kept looking around nervously, and finally said, "We didn't bring a gun. We'd better not run into a grizzly."

Louis grinned. He never seemed to worry much about bears. In fact, I think he actually enjoyed having the big bears around. While I cleaned dishes, Louis swung off on his crutches and disappeared into the trees. After a time I wondered where he had gone, and followed the little holes made by his crutches. He had turned off from the old road and followed a muddy game trail. I trotted along, thinking that the rubber tips of his crutches must have been smoking. Then I realized where he had headed. Louis was the perennial prospector, and had headed toward a mountain rock slide.

As I followed his trail, I saw fresh, foot-long, grizzly tracks. What a time to have a grizzly near—with a crippled husband, and no rifle. I caught up with Louis pounding a rock with his crutch. I herded him back to the boat. He protested, but I didn't relax my vigilance until we were aboard the boat and had paddled into the middle of the slough. There Louis removed several rocks from his pockets. "Look. Quartz, with some galena."

"How much silver?"

"Oh, about one or two ounces per ton."

"Pooh. That wouldn't make a mine."

Louis laughed. "Moose tracks in the snow won't make soup either, but if you follow them long enough you can eat steaks."

As the day waned, Louis caught more fish. I was netting a big whitefish for him when, nearby, we heard two shots from a heavy rifle. A pause, then came three more shots.

Was Billy in trouble?

Louis said, "He's probably shot a moose."

"All those shots for a moose? Not Billy," I said, grabbing a paddle. We didn't want the noise of the outboard now. As we moved up the slough, Billy's canoe shot out of a cove. He saw us and came alongside. Louis teased, "How about giving us some moose ribs?"

Billy laughed and shook his head. "No moose. Shoot grizzly bear."

"Was he big?" Louis asked, thinking of the grizzly tracks we had seen.

"Sure. Big. Track'n moose, me. Hear little kid moose holler like hell. He come run'n damn fast. Watch'm me. Behind come grizzly. That kid moose sure goin' to die. Pretty soon grizzly get'n closer. Shoot quick, me. Bear he fall over. Get up. Shoot, shoot. Bear he dead."

"Well, you skin him out and I'll sell the hide for you and make you a rich man," Louis offered.

That fishing trip was the most satisfying jaunt that Louis and I enjoyed that spring. A few days afterward, Louis' arm started to pain him. After several days of increasing discomfort, we drove to Mayo to see Dr. Clark.

While Louis was at the hospital, I went to the post office. Three hunters had written, thanking me for booking them for hunts during the coming fall. Now we had two 20-day hunts scheduled, with two hunters booked for each hunt. Louis thought he shouldn't try to hunt any more than four clients this season.

I walked over to see Mrs. Reynolds, and we were busily chatting when a telephone call came for me from the hospital matron. "Mrs. Brown, your husband would like to see you as soon as possible."

I found Louis staring blankly at the wall, and I knew he was fighting to control himself before talking to me. Finally, he looked at me with an expression of total defeat. "I have to have another operation. Something is wrong with the wire they used during the operation on my arm, and it isn't healing. This time they have to put a rod down the bone."

"Also," he said in a low, upset voice, his face downcast, "they can't take the casts off as soon as they thought. Maybe not until next winter."

Jack's Solution

Louis' news was almost more than I could cope with. First, I thought of all the suffering he had endured. Now he had to endure more, and he would have to spend more time in the hated hospital. Then, I realized, I would have to care for the horses again by myself.

"Oh, Louis," was all I could say, as I burst into tears. After a time we sat and stared miserably at one another. Then I had a sudden chilling thought: we had spent most of the deposit money from the four hunters. Clearly, Louis would be unable to guide in the fall. Would we both land in jail for embezzlement?

I was desperately trying to think of something encouraging to say when old Jack called, "I hear'n what you said. I know exactly how you feel. Doc says he can't cut off my leg 'til summer. Has to build me up first or something.

"Say, Louie, looks like you'n me be grounded this hunt'n season, but just never mind. Them wild critters better watch their hides come next year."

Fighting to keep the fear from my voice, I told the old prospector, "Yes, but Jack, we have hunters booked, and now Louis can't guide them, and . . . ."

I stopped, aghast that I was telling this poor old fellow our troubles.

Jack lit a pipe, clearly thinking. "Well, I don't see that's so bad. Any woman that kin snowshoe after horses when it's seventy six below like Louie told me you done kin sure handle a hunt'n party. And I think you should take that hunt'n party to my valley!"

He blew a smoke ring to give time for his suggestion to sink in. My mind whirled. It was true that the idea had gone through my mind, but it seemed so preposterous and frightening that I had refused to think about it. I knew only too well that it took a man like Louis to supervise the Indian guides. And it was my husband's vast knowledge of the wilderness and the habits of big game that made his hunts so successful.

And my qualifications? A girl's finishing school. In that school there were no lessons on how to cope with the tough trophy trails of the Yukon. Also, when I was born, the Creator made a mistake in installing my wiring. My sense of direction is nil. Once my sister and I arranged to meet in the lingerie department of a large store. I got lost. When she found me she said, "Good Lord, and you plan to marry a guide and live in the wilderness?"

"He's a good tracker!" I said, in defense.

There were other complications. I couldn't tell a moose track from that of a cow. I couldn't start a fire without diesel oil or kerosene. However, I could cook.

I looked at Louis. His face was turned firmly to the wall. I looked at Jack as he thought about his plan to put me in charge of a big game hunt in the Yukon.

"That sounds wonderful, Jack."

"Thought so myself," Jack agreed.

Louis remained silent.

Jack knocked the ashes from his pipe and pressed more tobacco into the bowl. "Fire me up again, then go down to the mining recorder and get me a map while I soft'n up your old man."

I hurriedly pecked Louis on the cheek and dashed into town. Gordon McIntyre, the mining recorder and magistrate, rolled up the maps I wanted and handed them to me. I went on to Mrs. Reynolds' home.

Ruth Kerbs, a schoolteacher I had met, was there. She loved horses and the out-of-doors. Once she had asked me if she could accompany Louis and me on one of our hunts to sketch the fantastic wilderness scenery of the Yukon. I had given her a lukewarm reply.

Assuming a nonchalant air I didn't really feel, I said, "I've just decided to take the hunting party out myself this year."

Ruth reacted violently, and squealed, "I'm going with you. You never know what kind of hunters you might have."

Mrs. Reynolds arrived carrying her silver tea service. "The sportsmen I've seen have been mostly doctors and lawyers."

"Or millionaires," I added feebly.

"Dolores, you've just hired yourself a cook!" Ruth shrieked.

"Ruth, are you serious? You'd really risk your neck to go with me on this hunt?"

"I was never more serious. You don't mind taking me?"

"No," I said, thinking, "there'll be plenty of cooking and other work. And you do know how to ride."

Mrs. Reynolds suggested, gently, "Ruth, you'd better get George to loan you his rifle and teach you how to use it."

We drank tea, and I hurriedly left, headed back to the hospital. I was astonished to find the entire men's ward involved in planning my hunt. Advice came like hailstones. More amazing, Louis was sitting up listening to Old Jack planning the hunt. The old prospector was like a general planning a military campaign.

When I produced the maps, every patient who could navigate clustered around Jack's bed. Jack spread a map over his knees and looked down with his sightless eyes. "Don, you put my finger on the lake then shut up. I know my valley, blindfolded."

I looked at Louis with a sad look, but the pathos of that old man remembering "his" valley didn't seem to bother him or any of the others.

Jack's finger crept along the shoreline and stopped at the south end. "Pitch your tents here. There's a big gnarled spruce tree and . . . ."

"That's a good idea, Jack," Henry Bell agreed. "If a grizzly stumbles into camp there'll be a tree handy to climb!"

"Yeh," Ken Allen said, "and if the bear charges, just ram your hand down his throat. Grab him by the tail and turn him wrong side out so he'll charge the other way. Ha ha . . . ."

Jack barked, "If ya ain't goin' to be serious, then git back to your beds."

"Aw, Jack, we was only kidd'n."

"Ya damn fools. Can't you see Mrs. Brown ain't exactly specialized in hunt'n parties, and ya might scare hell out of her."

"Well, Jack, why not just let the guides run it?" Henry asked.

"And do the cookin'?" Jack glared. "Ya saphead. Them *cheechako* (greenhorn) hunters ain't goin' to live on bum guts and charred moose ribs. Besides, somebody's gotta see they gets up in the morn'n and gits started."

Scotty bristled, "You got those Indians all wrong, Jack. Some of them Indians are better cooks than any damn white man—and a good Indian'll get up earlier than most white men I know."

Jack had Andy Jonas mark the trail from Keno to his valley. From there the line zigzagged to a salt lick, through a pass, and then continue up one valley and down another. Different species of game fed in different places along the trail, and Jack had Andy mark these in.

Don Buyack snorted, "I'd sure as hell get lost in that tangle."

"She's gonna stay right in camp," Jack said.

"Well, if you get lost, just remember the moss grows on the north side of a tree, and the white powder on the poplars is thickest on the south or sunny side."

"She's stay'n in camp," Jack thundered, and I agreed with him one hundred percent.

Scotty edged up to me. "Don't tell the Indian guides noth'n. They don't like to be bossed by a woman. 'Specially one that don't know noth'n bout hunt'n."

Don Buyak warned, "Check the hunters and see they don't keep shells in the chambers of their rifles so you don't have a gun accident."

I looked at Louis. He smiled wanly. "It'll only be for the first 20 days. I'll get Fred Farleen to take over the last hunt. He says he's coming back from his prospect about August 18th."

"That will be fine," I said, thinking that surely I could last that long.

Louis had been thinking about the Indian guides. "Lonny Johnny is your best bet for a guide. He's been with me the longest, and he knows the ropes. Doc Johnny can be your second guide. Gordon Mervyn should be your wrangler—I started training him for that job when he was a boy. Also, he's the only man in the outfit who can shoe a horse."

"Should I send for more horseshoes?"

"Yes. And you'd better check on the hobbles and halters so you'll know how many to order. I'll be down in a couple of weeks and start getting the pack outfit together."

Dr. Clark came in, smiling. "Mrs. Brown, I heard some of the plans. I'll fix you up with a good first aid kit."

"Put in plenty of bandages," I laughed.

The meeting broke up when Dr. Clark looked at Louis and said, "Well, what say we get that arm fixed?"

"Ready," said Louis, reluctantly, as he swung his legs over the side of the bed.

"Dolores, you'd better send for your chief guide's license right away."

"CHIEF GUIDE. ME?"

"Why not? You're going to be the boss."

Louis hobbled after Dr. Clark. At the door of the surgery he turned and called, "Better learn how to tie a diamond hitch, too."

I groaned. I detest knots, especially confusing and complicated ones— like the diamond hitch, which is used to hold a pack on a horse.

I returned to Mrs. Reynolds' home, borrowed pen and paper, and wrote a letter to the Yukon Game Department, applying for a license.

I had postmistress Mabel McIntyre register the letter. She has the most adorable chuckle. "Pretty important, eh?"

"About the most important letter I ever wrote. Please, Mabel, when the reply comes give it to Ruth and she'll bring it down to me."

I met Ruth at the Chateau Cafe, and after we had coffee, she drove me to the Indian Village. A swarm of Indian children located Lonny Johnny for me. He was a small Fort McPherson Indian, one of Louis' favorites.

"Lonny, would you be one of my guides for the hunt this fall?" I asked.

He leaned against a tree leisurely, and looked at me through half-closed eyes. With a haughty grunt he asked, "You kill'm grizzly?"

"No. But I killed a moose once. He was big."

Lonny sneered. He made it clear that because I had killed a mere moose didn't qualify me to give him orders.

"Louie my boss," he grunted.

"Yes, I know. Louis says you're plenty smart. That's why I want you for my guide."

"Louie kill plenty grizzly."

"I know," I said, impatiently.

"Louie all same Indian."

I turned in exasperation and rolled my eyes at Ruth as a sign that I had given up. Ruth clutched my arm and gave Lonny her sweetest smile. "Why, Lonny, you aren't going to turn down a job that gives you five more dollars a day than the other guides."

Lonny immediately began to take an interest. He looked at me for confirmation.

"For heaven's sake, Ruth," I stammered, wondering if this leap in salary would bankrupt us. Then I remembered that Lonny was the only Indian guide we knew who had been to Jack's valley.

"Yes, of course, Lonny. You get five dollars more."

As we climbed into the car, Ruth said, "I like his enthusiasm."

"Never mind about Lonny. He's loyal to Louis, and he's a good guide. But Ruth, please don't raise the salaries of the others."

Doc Johnny and Gordon Mervyn agreed to go if Lonny went. I hoped Lonny would keep his mouth shut about his increased pay.

Ruth drove me back to the ranch and promised to deliver the letter from the Game Department when it arrived. A few days later old Billy came over for a visit. He stood watching with interest as I tottered on the top rail of the corral with two hands full of rope. I was trying to tie it into a diamond hitch.

One of our gentlest and most patient mares, Queen, stood quietly, loaded with a pair of pack boxes. Atop the boxes were two 20-pound sacks of cooking oats. Billy rather irritated me, standing around doing nothing, so after completing the knot, I tossed him the long end of the rope as I had seen Louis do hundreds of times with his wranglers. "Put one foot on Queen's rump and pull as hard as you can," I told him.

To Billy's credit, he followed instructions. He is a very big and strong Indian. He braced his moccasin against Queen and gave a mighty pull. My diamond hitch unraveled like a piece of crochet, and Billy's contact with the ground must have rattled his teeth. He leaped up, and without a word, stalked down the trail, his dignity shattered.

Next day Billy's dignity had recovered enough for him to return, for he was curious. "Why you pack horse?"

"Well, Billy," I explained, "Louis won't be able to guide the hunters, so I'm going to do it."

"Where you go?"

"Jack's valley," I told him, describing the location.

Billy thought that over, then decided to reveal a horrible fact. "Old people say bad wolf that place. Big spots on 'em. Very bad. Eat lots Indian people."

"Oh, Billy, you probably mean one of those prehistoric animals. They died out long ago."

Billy still didn't think my going hunting without Louis was a good idea. "Maybe white hunter bad."

"I'm sure the hunters are nice."

Billy snorted. "Lots white men look all right, talk all right. No good inside."

Daily, I listened for the sound of Ruth's car. I began to worry, and I wondered what the Game Department would do if I went hunting without a guide's license. Late one afternoon Ruth drove up and braked to a sudden stop. She leaped from the car, waving a letter. "It's come. It's come."

I tore open the envelope. It held my license!

"Oh, Ruth, I got it."

The license, issued by the Yukon Department of Game, authorized me to act as guide to any persons for the purpose of hunting in the Ogilvie, Wind, and Bonnet Plume areas of the Yukon Territory. I was staggered to realize that Canada was willing to trust more than 6,000 square miles of her virgin wilderness, filled with hordes of moose, Dall sheep, caribou, and grizzly bears, to a girl educated in a private school for young ladies in Walla Walla, Washington.

Ruth smiled, "I'm glad that was good news, for I bring bad tidings."

"Very bad?"

Ruth nodded. "Do you want it in small doses, or . . . ."

"I take my castor oil in one big gulp."

"Lonny Johnny is in the hospital with tuberculosis of the bone, and is being sent to Edmonton. Doc Johnny has gone fire fighting and won't be back. Gordon Mervyn is keeping Lonny company in the men's ward with something seriously wrong with his neck."

I leaned heavily on the corral rails. "Ruth, if you say something is wrong with you, I'll scream."

"Not a chance. I'm ready to make this hunt if it takes my last breath."

Ruth left, and I sat on the fence watching the horses, wishing they had all been born with iron shoes on their hoofs. The biggest blow had been the loss of Gordon Mervyn, since he was the only one who could shoe the horses.

I sat thinking. Red had been the only difficult one to shoe: he had always tried to climb the barn walls. But poor Red was gone. Thinking of him made me choke up, and I wondered if he was now galloping his way through celestial pastures.

Queen nibbled my fingers. "Queen, you owe your life to me. You wouldn't try to kick my head off if I tried to shoe you? Or would you?"

As I sat petting Queen, the thought kept growing that maybe I could shoe a horse. There is nothing to it: you file their hoofs like I did my fingernails, and then nail a shoe on.

I got down and found a horseshoeing rasp, buckled on Louis' chaps, and collected the shoeing hammer and nails. I coaxed Queen to put her hoof on a stump, then I started filing. Queen rolled her eyes around and started to teeter.

"You're going to get a new set of shoes whether you like it or not," I told her.

Queen refused to stand still, so I worked her hoof between my legs as I'd seen Louis do. Perspiration gushed into my eyes, and my back sagged lower and lower. Suddenly, it dawned on me—I was practically holding up a 1,400-pound packhorse.

"Queen," I yelled, jabbing her in the ribs, "You're leaning on me."

I found it impossible to keep her from weaving, so I decided to omit the pedicure, and just nail on the shoe. With the hammer, I started to drive a nail through a horseshoe into the bottom of her hoof. She peered around at me wild-eyed, then reared. I jerked her back down. Next, I tried to yank out a nail I had hammered in crooked.

Finally, her patience used up, Queen flung herself back, broke the halter rope, and lost her balance. She toppled on her side, knocking me down. Staggering to her feet, she snorted and fled down the trail, eyes rolling, and the loose horseshoe flapping with every bound!

Conqueror of Grave Digger

Ruth drove Louis home a few days after my atttempt to shoe Queen. When they arrived, I was trying to catch Queen for the umpteenth time to finish the shoeing job. She wouldn't come close even for oats, and she was much too wise to go into the corral. Ruth jumped from the car, and Louis slowly climbed out, maneuvering on his crutches. "Give us a cup of tea and we'll help you catch that old nag," said Ruth brightly.

Louis had news. He had picked up the mail. "One of your hunters has cancelled, so you'll need only one guide for the first hunt. Harry Baum at Pelly River says he'll go. Harry is a top tracker. His only problem is that he thinks a horse should go any place a moose can travel."

Never forgetting my own capacity for getting lost, I considered Harry's tracking skill his most valuable asset.

Louis finished his tea and reached for his crutches. "Horses have to leave in a week if they're to get to Jack's valley in time for the hunt. Our problem now is to find a good wrangler. Come on. Let's get busy."

As we left the cabin, Queen, a full hundred yards away, sidled off. "What's wrong with Queen? She's limping," Louis asked. "She must have gotten kicked," I mumbled.

We took strategic places. Queen cropped grass as if we didn't exist. I crept up on her with a halter behind my back. She distrustfully eyed me, then snorted wildly and galloped off. Ruth waved her new white western hat, and Louis made a fence with his crutches. That turned her. Suddenly Queen stopped, tossed her head, then stood looking down the road in the direction of loud yodeling. I shook my head to clear my ears. It *was* yodeling, the kind some cowboys do.

Then we saw a cowboy hat coming down the road. When it neared, we saw a big shining silver belt buckle and a pair of cowboy boots. All three of us stood gaping at this Texas-like display in dog-team country.

Queen saw her opportunity and dashed past us and almost past the cowboy, for that, sure enough, is what wore the hat, boots, and belt-buckle. The cowboy, seeing the escaping horse, suddenly whirled a lariat that neatly settled around Queen's neck. She meekly allowed him to lead her to the corral fence, where I slipped the halter on, and securely tied her.

The cowboy swung the saddle he had been carrying on his back onto the railing of the corral. He was a thin, dark-skinned, handsome young Indian. He leaned lazily against the corral and regarded us with amusement. His eyes and grin seemed to say, "You couldn't catch that old plug of a horse, but I could."

Louis recovered first. "Who are you?"

"New wrangler."

"But you're just a kid," Louis blurted. "What's your name, and how old are you?"

"Lucky John." The boy drew himself up, "Twenty-one years old." He said it in a way that was a challenge for us to deny it. He appeared to be about sixteen.

Louis cleared his throat. "You've probably heard we need a wrangler. But it has to be someone with experience. We need someone who can do a man's job. I'm afraid you can't handle it."

A fleeting look of disappointment crossed the boy's face. I hurriedly invited, "Come in for a cup of tea." Lucky grabbed his saddle and followed. Ruth whispered, "Another adolescent with Wild West indigestion."

Lucky ignored my suggestion to leave his saddle outside. Instead he lugged it into the cabin and dumped it on the floor. Then, as if patiently humoring the aged, he nonchalantly sank into the saddle. In the next moment all hell broke loose. With dark eyes flashing, coal black hair flying, legs flying, and arms flailing, Lucky vigorously raked his jingling spurs over the floor. "Rid'n Gray Ghost," he yelled as he twisted, leaped, and bounced the saddle across the room.

In another moment, "Rid'n Black Snake now," he shrilled. Pictures tilted on the walls, and dishes rattled in the cupboard. Our incipient cowboy slammed into a chair and knocked it over. "Now rid'n One Way Ticket." Louis was laughing so hard that tears came to his eyes. I was puzzled about the horses our wild rider was forking until Louis managed to explain, "Those are the worst buckers on the rodeo circuit."

Ruth and I dashed about, grabbing breakables. "Gonna break ole Grave Digger," whooped our leaping saddle bum. By all odds, Grave Digger was the most ferocious bucker, and he almost unseated our gallant cowboy. However, by skilled horsemanship, Lucky rode him to the finish. We drew a sigh of relief when he dismounted. But Lucky, encouraged by our enraptured attention, climbed back on his saddle, and proceeded to demonstrate how Casey Tibbs, Jim Shoulders, Bob Schild, and other rodeo greats handled their broncs. Spurring, and fanning his hat, Lucky gave us a running account of their every technique. When he finally rose from his almost-smoking saddle, he gave the impression that he had just won top money for the day. When Louis' laughter ended, he said "Lucky, you're quite a boy!"

Lucky wasn't through with us yet. He was going to cinch this job. He leveled a second barrel at us. "Lucky work for Mike Nolan."

Louis raised his eyebrows. Mike Nolan, an ex-Mounty, was a big game outfitter who operated out of Marsh Lake. Lucky launched into a detailed account of his work with Nolan. "C'n tie basket and barrel hitches, me. Squaw and diamond hitch too. Can . . . ."

"Can you shoe a horse?" I asked, looking at Queen through the window.

"Can Lucky shoe a horse?" he mimicked, and stalked out the door. Louis grabbed his crutches and speedily followed.

Ruth sighed, "That kid has the biggest case of Western Fever I've ever seen."

"I wonder if he could handle our pancake-eating pack-string?" I mused.

When Louis returned, he was wearing a big grin. "That kid sure did a neat job of shoeing Queen. Tomorrow he'll shoe the rest of the horses. Right now we'd better take him across the river in the scow to pick up Dan and Baldy."

Ruth left, prophesying, "He's a big tease, and he'll drive us crazy."

The scow was large enough to hold a dozen horses. Nevertheless, Dan and Baldy displayed an unholy fear of it. They both kicked and fought as Lucky dragged them aboard and tied them securely. Our new wrangler worried about Louis, sitting in the stern, running the outboard motor unprotected from the heels of the two plunging horses. He nailed some 2 × 4s across the scow, fencing Louis in, then he stood between the two frightened animals, firmly gripping their halters. At the sound of the outboard motor, they lunged and plunged, lifting skinny little Lucky up and down as if they were mashing potatoes with him. Afraid the boy would be hurt, Louis yelled, "Come back here with me."

When the scow was halfway across the river Dan broke his halter rope and plunged into the river, quickly followed by Baldy. Both were strong swimmers, and Louis used the outboard-powered scow to herd them to the home shore.

At supper, Lucky asked if I liked Scotty Stevenson, Curly Vance, Hank Williams, Webb Pierce, and Jimmy Rodgers. "Never heard of them," I answered. "Were they big winners on bucking horses?"

Lucky plopped his fork down and gave me a hopeless look. He sighed, trying to resign himself. "Mrs. Brown, this Hank Williams." Then he threw his head back and sang snatches of songs.

"Oh. Then they're singers."

"Yes, Mrs. Brown. Jimmy Rodgers knows forty-two yodels." And Lucky proceeded to demonstrate all forty-two.

I wondered how I was going to endure Jimmy Rodgers. My tastes tend toward the classics. While I was washing dishes, Louis read a prospector's manual, and Lucky wandered around, curious about everything in the cabin. Hearing a *swish, swish, swishing* sound, I whirled and caught Lucky spraying himself with some of my imported cologne. I snatched it from him.

"That's very expensive," I glared.

He shrugged and borrowed a pencil and notebook from Louis and asked him to step outside. When Louis returned he grinned at me, "Your wrangler wants you to order some of that good smelling stuff for him. Seems he's engaged to a Mary Rabbit over at Carmacks. It's to be a love offering."

"What do you mean *my* wrangler?" I asked.

"Well, you're running the hunt," Louis replied, his eyes dancing with devilment. I changed the subject. "Stockings would be more practical," I snapped. "Do you think stockings more romantic?" Louis asked, with his innocent expression.

As the days wound down closer to departure day, Lucky followed Louis' about on his thumping crutches, and the colt, Copper, devotedly trotted behind Lucky. Every time Louis started a job, Lucky, anxious to help, took over. Occasionally, I saw him suddenly stop work and stare dreamily into space. Then he would madly scribble into his notebook. One day I asked, "Louis, what in heaven's name is Lucky writing in that notebook?"

Louis grinned. "Oh, he's composing songs for your hunt. Wants to be a second Jerome Kerns or Jimmy Rodgers, Yukon style."

"Well, make him stop right now."

"I can't squelch a budding genius."

"Louis, have you thought about another guide for the second hunt?"

"Yep. Lucky is writing for his dad to come."

We completed plans. Lucky and Harry Baum, the guide, were to take the pack train with equipment, food, and supplies to Jack's valley. Ruth and I would charter a plane and fly to the valley with our first client, Meade Ion, of Grosse Pointe, Michigan.

On departure day, Lucky loaded the horses, and, since neither of us had a driver's license, Louis awkwardly climbed into the driver's seat, painfully adjusted his heavy casts, and headed down the road. It required three trips to get the horses and gear to Keno City, start of the trail. Harry Baum was to meet us at Keno City at seven o'clock in the morning. Ruth had driven him to Mayo, and he said he would ride up with Joe Nelson. Louis and Lucky saddled and packed the horses, and they were ready on time. Ten o'clock came, but there was still no sign of Harry. Storm clouds threatened as they rolled up behind Keno Hill. The air was still. Not a leaf stirred.

"Where in the hell is Harry?" asked Louis.

We ate lunch. Two o'clock came. No Harry. Louis drove me to the Silver Queen Hotel and I telephoned Mayo. Oliver Hutton hadn't seen Harry, and neither had Wilfred Gordon. In desperation, I called the Royal Canadian Mounted Police. "Do you happen to know where Harry Baum is?"

"I sure do. We have him in jail," answered Constable Cruthers.

"In jail! He's supposed to guide our packtrain out for a long hunt!"

"Don't worry about Harry. He'll be out in ten days."

"TEN DAYS! He's supposed to be here right now! The horses are packed and waiting for him," I yelled, trying not to become hysterical.

There was a long pause on the other end of the line. Finally Constable Cruthers said, "This is Sunday. The magistrate may be out to Mayo Lake, fishing. If you can find him and he'll hold a quick trial and you pay the fine, we might be able to let Harry go." It was my turn to think. I realized that Harry must have decided to have a big party the night before leaving for the long hunt.

I asked, "Is Harry able to sit on a horse?"

"Oh, yes, Mrs. Brown. We took him in last night."

"We'll be in Mayo as soon as we can get there," I hung the receiver up with a bang.

When Louis and I got back, two of the horses had broken loose and headed home. Lucky had gone after them. Ruth had to stay to be sure that none of the Indian children gathered around the horses were kicked or trampled. Louis and I wearily climbed back into the truck, hoping that the threatening storm had kept the magistrate at home.

We were halfway to Mayo when the storm broke. Sheets of water swept across the road. Lightning flashes blinded us. Rain mixed with sleet flooded the windshield so heavily the wipers couldn't keep up. We skidded and slid down the narrow, winding dirt/gravel road. With his one good arm, Louis fought the wheel to keep the truck on the road. His face was pale and drawn. The casts on his leg and arm were rubbing him painfully.

At last, weary and worried, we arrived at the police barracks. I jumped out and sloshed through the mud. The doors were locked, but I caught a glimpse of Harry peeking out between the bars. For a wild moment I considered attempting a jail break and yanking Harry out.

Then I splashed to the Silver Inn Cafe and found Constable Cruthers there drinking coffee. He was courteous and concerned, but the law made it impossible for him to release Harry without a trial before the magistrate. I returned to the barracks with Cruthers and from there telephoned the magistrate, Gordon McIntyre. "This is Mrs. Brown. We're in trouble, and I wonder if you can help us?"

"What kind of trouble?"

I explained the whole miserable situation.

"Be right over," he said.

Louis went in for the trial. I went to the cafe and drank several cups of coffee to calm my nerves. Louis came out ten dollars lighter, followed by a sheepish Harry. He grinned, "Hello, Boss." I couldn't believe my ears. He had called me Boss! I forgave him everything.

By the time we arrived back at Keno City it was too late to start on the trail. Lucky had caught the two runaways. He and Harry unpacked the horses. We all stayed at the Silver Queen Hotel that night. Drunks paraded up and down the hall, shouting jolly insults to their pals. We heard a chair crash over someone's unlucky head, and the sound of shattering glass drifted through with monotonous regularity.

Near dawn we gave up trying to sleep. After Louis had collected Lucky and Harry, we went to the Sourdough Cafe and routed out the owner, Old Massa. He was a jovial little Japanese who had arrived in Keno City in the early days. While we decided what to order, he leaned on the counter and told Ruth how in his first years he had had to shoot caribou and moose to get meat for his cafe.

Massa soon carried out huge platters of ham and eggs. We had barely started to eat, when we heard a loud whinny. Ruth jumped up and looked out the window. "Another horse is loose!"

I whirled around, expecting to see Copper coming through the door. But it wasn't a horse. Ruth gave me a sharp nudge and I turned to see what she was trying to tell me. My eyes opened wide and my mouth flew open. Standing on the top step of the doorway leading to the kitchen stood a tall, dark-haired women—in her nightgown.

Giving another shrill whinny, the woman pranced around inside the horseshoe-shaped counter and stopped in front of Louis. "Are you the owner of that beautiful stallion?"

Louis, in shock and embarrassed, could only nod.

"Oh, he's a virile horse. So much spirit, so much...life."

She pranced off with arched neck, making another circle of the counter. Harry and Lucky sat frozen and staring, their forks full of egg halfway to their mouths.

Ruth hissed, "Madam Zoom."

Madam Zoom! She was a famous (or infamous) Dawson City madam, well known throughout the Territory for her many talents.

The nightgown-wearing madam high-stepped over to Lucky. Before the surprised boy could protest, she bent down and ate the egg from his fork. Nonchalantly reaching to Harry's plate, she nibbled on his toast and washed it down with Louis' coffee. She wrinkled her nose at my orange marmalade, and finished Ruth's strawberry jam on my last piece of toast.

Leisurely, and with complete unconcern, she consumed our breakfasts while we all sat like a bunch of dumbbells. When finished, she gave another loud whinny and pranced out of sight.

Lucky broke the spell by indignantly yelling, "Hell. That crazy lady. She should pay for breakfast. She ate all!"

We left, still bemused by Madam Zoom's strange behavior. Some of the jokes Louis cracked while supervising the packing of the horses won't be repeated here. While making a last check with my list, I stopped dead in my tracks. Our young wrangler sat in his saddle with a guitar across his lap.

"Lucky. Where did you get that thing?"

He grinned. "Borrowed."

"But you can't wrangle horses while you're carrying a guitar."

Lucky laughed and gave the strings a twang.

When all was ready the horses strung out between Harry, in the lead, and Lucky, in the rear. They started smartly, the horses tossing their heads, eager to be on the trail. Harry whipped out his harmonica and started a tune. He swayed in the saddle, keeping time. Lucky banged the strings of his borrowed guitar and sang:

"Go'n big game hunting, Harry and I

Over t'ose mountains high in the sky

Look out you rams, we'll roast your ribs

Look out you moose, and little kids

Look out you caribou wit' your shovels

Look out you grizzly, you're in for trouble

Cause Harry and I go'n to watch you die

We're wolves on your trail. Bye, bye."

Lucky turned in his saddle and waved the guitar. I could see his white teeth as he grinned. Then both Indians threw back their heads and howled like a pair of wolves.

Louis grinned. "Jerome Kern just rolled over in his grave."

I shuddered.

Ruth groaned, "I wonder if we'll ever see them again?"

Hell No, She's a Guide!

O ur client for the first hunt, Meade Ion, of Grosse Pointe, Michigan, arrived. He was jovial and friendly. When Louis informed him that I was to guide his hunt all he said was, "Fine with me."

Louis liked him instantly. Ruth and I did too, to our great relief. It's difficult to judge a person through correspondence, and we had been worried. Even old Billy said, "That man, him good inside."

Louis took Meade to meet some Yukon pioneers, while Ruth and I went to the hospital to say good-bye to Jack. We could tell that he would like to have been going with us. The old blind prospector tried to be jolly, but the sadness showed through.

I tried hard to swallow the lump in my throat. "Jack, what shall I bring you back from your valley?"

"Jist come back safe is all I ask."

"There must be something. Ptarmigan? Sheep meat?"

Jack shook his head. Ruth looked at him with misty eyes.

"Jack, I'm going to paint a picture of your valley for you."

"Now, that would be nice," he said, fumbling for his pipe.

Seeing his groping hand, Ruth suddenly remembered he was blind. Jack was so cheerful and normal, that we tended to forget that fact.

"Maybe, Jack, you'd rather have a pretty rock."

"Nope. Rather have a picture. But put gobs of paint where that old gnarled spruce is, and where the Indian head rock be."

A nurse stopped to check on Jack. She brightly commented, "Mrs. Brown, I hear you're going to be the grease cook on the hunt into Jack's valley."

"Hell no, she's the guide!" Jack roared. The nurse stared at me in amazement and said, "Oh," and left, clearly confused.

I took Jack's hand, "Thank you for letting me hunt in your valley." Jack gripped tightly. "You mind my word. Keep a sharp eye out for them grizzlies. The bears in there hev been crossed with a polar bear—or the devil!"

"I'll be careful. And, Jack, while I'm gone, would you sort of look after Louis? See that he doesn't worry?"

"Damn right I will. I heard about that fool driving his truck with all that cement on his leg and arm. Think I'll go down and cook for him so I kin keep m' eye on 'im."

Jack sat up straight and puffed furiously on his pipe. Choking back tears, Ruth and I said hasty good-byes and dashed out to her car. Ruth said, "That brave, blind old dear."

Early next morning hunter Meade Ion, Ruth, Louis, and I watched Pat Callison's float-equipped Cessna land on the Stewart River at Mayo. While Pat loaded his plane, Louis gave me last-minute instructions. "Use your binoculars a lot to help Harry spot game. Don't forget to check the hides and capes every day to see that the edges haven't curled. Have Lucky build racks to keep the saddles and blankets off the ground."

Pat yelled, "Let's go, Dolores."

I felt my heart was going to break. Would I ever see Louis again? How was he going to carry water from the river? How was he going to chop wood? How was he . . .?

Louis hugged and kissed me. "Happy hunting, Honey. Remember, it's only for twenty days."

He noticed that I was beginning to cloud up. "Yukon guides don't cry!" he warned, lifting my chin with his fist.

"Louis, if I don't come back, will you keep my silver tea set polished?"

"Honey, when you come back you'll have to wear sunglasses to look at it."

Ruth and I climbed aboard the plane and sprawled on top of the duffel. Meade sat in front with pilot Pat. I waved good-bye to Louis, who looked alone and pathetic, leaning heavily on his crutches. Pat opened the throttle and sent the silver plane skimming across the water. It lifted into the air. I was fascinated to be able to peer down at the tops of spruce trees and at winding streams.

Pat banked the plane and pointed. "Moose," he called. A cow moose feeding in a slough raised her head as the plane passed.

Meade leaned back, "Dolores, I want a real grizzly."

"You'll get one," I shouted over the roar of the engine. If I could have foreseen just how my hunter was going to bag his grizzly, I would have told Pat to turn the plane back to Mayo. We flew over platter valleys filled with spaghetti-sprawled streams. Below us were great mountain ridges etched with spiderweb caribou trails. Here and there we saw emerald lakes embedded among the white peaks. In about an hour we flew into a snowstorm. The clouds were thick, swirling, black. Somewhere below was Jack's valley. Pat circled, and the clouds grew blacker. Suddenly, the darkness gave way to a dazzling opening, and a shimmering blue lake sparkled below. It was as though the gates of heaven had opened. Pat dived the plane through and, as if on a magic carpet, he leveled the plane over paradise. Jack's valley was bright with sunshine.

Unfortunately, there was no camp, no horses, no wrangler, no guide.

Ruth and I flattened our faces against the windows and prayed. "Please circle again, Pat," I begged. "They've got to be here somewhere."

How embarrassing it would be to land a hunter to hunt where there were no tents, no stove, nothing to eat, no horses, no guide. Finally Pat drew the line. "Dolores, if I make one more circle around this valley, I won't have enough gas to get back to Mayo."

He made a final turn. My ears popped in the descent, and the sleek plane skimmed above the lake and the floats kissed the silvery water. As Pat taxied toward the spruce-lined shore, Ruth pointed. "Horses," she screeched. Harry, Lucky, and the packtrain were just arriving.

Pat beached the plane. Remembering Louis' advice, I focused my 12 × 50 binoculars on the surrounding country, and almost jumped out of my shoepacks. Trembling with excitement, I pointed out three bull caribou to Meade. He was delighted.

"This is really something! Wonderful! Within five minutes, I see game!"

Ruth finished tossing our duffel to the men, and, carrying her borrowed .300 Savage, climbed off the pontoons. Lucky warily eyed her. "You shoot horse, maybe?"

"I've never shot anything," Ruth snapped.

Lucky relieved Ruth of her rifle, opened the action, and found a cartridge in the chamber. "Sure as hell shoot somebody or horse, you keep shell in chamber like t'at!" Ruth deserved that tongue-lashing. As boss of the outfit, I turned my back and said nothing, figuring she would get the message.

I was disappointed to note that Lucky's borrowed guitar had survived the trip. Lucky helped Pat turn his plane around, and shoved him off. Soon the plane's engine hum faded into the distance, and we were alone and on our own in the deep wilderness of the Yukon.

As we stood on the shore, a speckled trout lazily surfaced in a feeding roll. Lucky saw Meade's excited stare, and suggested, "Doctor, maybe you catch fish?"

I took Lucky aside. "Mr. Ion is not a doctor."

"Mrs. Brown, Louie say make hunter happy. All white men like feel important," he said.

"You need spinner, Doctor," he called to Meade.

Meade laughed. "I'm afraid my profession doesn't warrant the title."

"You big shot just like doctor, all same," Lucky complimented.

Meade smiled. Lucky nudged me. "He like that doctor stuff."

We found Jack's gnarled spruce, and Harry and Lucky set up the cook tent beneath it. The side wall had a small tear, and Ruth was mending it when Lucky paused beside her. "My dad say, when woman carry needle and thread, they past forty years."

Ruth gritted her teeth. "And my dad say you're nothing but an insufferable teenager." Fire flashed in Lucky's eyes, and I hastily told him to put up the cook stove.

Ruth asked, "What shall I cook for supper? I can't think of a thing."

Already I was beginning to realize the scope of my responsibilities. Sparks were flying between Ruth and Lucky, and I had to soothe both of them. I had to organize a camp routine, and see that everyone did his job. On previous hunts, Louis had made all the decisions, and all I had to do was cook and help out wherever Louis pointed me.

"You'll have to look through the pack boxes and see what we have," I suggested. I searched for and found the folding table, and went to start a fire in the cook tent. There was no stove in the tent, and Lucky had disappeared. Ruth and I found the stove, and we were struggling to fit the stovepipe together when Lucky tossed back the tent flap and dropped six ptarmigan in Ruth's lap.

"Cook chicken for supper. Lucky, he hunter, not teenager."

Ruth ooh'd and aah'd. "Now I can make Chicken Terrapin. Now if only I had mushrooms."

"Lucky, I didn't hear any shots," I said.

Lucky smirked. "Don't need gun. Throw rocks."

I was amazed. That Indian kid was something. He had bagged our dinner by throwing rocks.

Harry arrived with the packhorse Dina, loaded with our duffel bags. While he and Lucky finished setting up the stove, Ruth and I explored. Ducks paddled in the creek. Ptarmigan whirred from the bushes. Blue bells grew in profusion, while halfway up the mountainsides leaves were turning to brilliant autumn hues. This was high country. There was no summer here—only spring, fall, and winter.

"Mushrooms!" Ruth yelled. "Look. All over the place." We filled our hats with large plump mushrooms. "Do you know about good or bad mushrooms?"

"I think that nothing poisonous grows in the Yukon," I reassured.

When we returned to camp, Meade was walking up the trail with a big string of fish. "How about fish and hot biscuits for breakfast?" he called, happily.

"Wonderful," I agreed. Then I turned to Lucky, "Please clean the fish."

Lucky gave me a smoldering look. "Lucky no squaw."

"Don't you know how to clean fish?" I asked, in exasperation.

Lucky mimicked, "Don't you know how to clean fish?"

Our young wrangler had no difficulty with the language when he wanted to needle. Otherwise he deliberately talked in the Indian shorthand that says so much in so few words.

I grabbed the fish and headed for the creek. Ruth followed. "Dolores," she whispered, "do as I do."

"What?" I asked, puzzled.

Ruth let out a peal of laughter. "Oh, Dolores, that's so funny." Then she laughed again. I stared at her, bewildered. Ruth jabbed my ribs and laughed louder. Suddenly, I caught on, and threw back my head and laughed loudly. Since neither of us had ever cleaned a fish before, we were soon laughing in earnest. Soon a familiar cowboy hat appeared above the willows.

"Go away, Lucky," Ruth yelled.

Lucky, beside himself with curiosity, came over, picked up a fish, slit it open with lightning speed, and had it cleaned almost before he had picked it up.

"Get out of here. This is squaw's work," Ruth told him. But Lucky sank on his heels and grabbed another fish. Ruth winked, and we sat back and told funny stories while Lucky finished cleaning the fish.

While Ruth sauteed two pans of mushrooms, I made a peach pie. After supper, Meade patted his stomach. "Ladies, that meal would have done credit to the Waldorf Astoria. Don't hesitate to make peach pie any time you feel like it. And Ruth, the ptarmigan and those mushrooms were delicious."

"There are a lot more mushrooms growing here," Ruth blurted. On his way out of the cook tent Meade stopped. "You picked them here? Can you tell poisonous from non-poisonous?"

"Oh, Dolores says nothing poisonous grows in the Yukon," Ruth glibly responded.

"I hope she's right," muttered our hunter as he made a quick exit.

Ruth and I were washing dishes when Lucky poked his head into the tent. "Mrs. Brown, Harry say he have belly ache." Ruth and I nervously looked at each other. Both of us were thinking how far we were from help.

"Lucky, bring Harry here at once," I ordered. Then to Ruth, "Help me find the first-aid kit." We couldn't find it. Instead, Ruth found a medicinal-looking bottle. "What's this?" "Horse medicine," I answered mechanically. Then, "In an emergency, do you suppose . . .?"

"It doesn't hurt a horse, does it?" Ruth asked, in quick understanding.

I remembered something from our mushroom-picking of the afternoon. "Ruth, two of the mushrooms looked different than the rest. We have to do something, just in case."

Ruth held the bottle near the flickering candle and read, "Dose according to size and age of animal."

Harry burst through the tent flaps, pushed by Lucky. "Harry, how much do you weigh, and how old are you?" I asked. He grunted. "I dunno. Big pain in belly."

Ruth continued to read the directions. "For cattle, 30 to 40 drops. Calves, sheep, or colts 3 to 5 drops. Horses 20 to 30 drops. Pigs 1 to 10 drops."

We all turned and looked speculatively at Harry. Lucky giggled, "All same big pig, Harry."

"Shut up. Can't you ever be serious? This may be life or death," Rush said testily.

Harry, who had never seen a pig in his life, nodded, "Big pig, me."

Ruth and I agreed on the dose for a calf, and Harry uneasily gulped it down and bolted. Lucky followed him strumming the guitar and singing:

"Mrs. Brown, I tell you no lie

Poor Harry go'n to die

Then everybody'll cry."

A pot lid zinged through the air. Lucky dodged, yelping with glee, and Ruth muttered, "I should have thrown the pot."

Neechemoos

Lucky's voice, accompanied by his twanging guitar, was loud, penetrating, raucous.

"Mrs. Brown, Mrs. Brown, I tell you no lie. Yodelaeo

Sandman, he forget me last night. Yodelaeo

My eyes stayed open I so scared. Yodelaeo

With eyes open, Lucky no sleep. Yodelaeo

See big track. Not moose track. Yodelaeo

Not sheep track. Not mouse. Yodelaeo

It so big I almost faint. Yodelaeo

It one bad grizzly track. Yodelaeo"

Ruth groaned. I drew the sleeping bag over my head. It was useless. There was no shutting out the exuberant serenade. "LUCKY!" I screamed. "Shut up and go to bed."

"Louie Brown say be nice to hunter, so Lucky make Doctor coffee," came Lucky's muffled response.

"Not in the middle of the night," I snapped.

Lucky hooted with laughter. "Oh, Mrs. Brown, it morning."

"Then go get the horses."

Shivering, Ruth and I fumbled into damp, cold clothes and staggered to the cook tent. A large pot of coffee danced on the hot stove. Ruth poured us a cup and took a quick sip.

"Never tell your wrangler he makes good coffee or he'll be unbearable," I warned Ruth. Finishing my coffee, I said, "I've dreaded today, wondering about Harry and if . . . ."

"Don't worry about your guide. I heard him last night."

"You did?"

"Yep. He was either gasping for his last breath, or he was snoring."

Ruth fried the fish while I made biscuits. She stuck her head out to announce breakfast, then drew back with relief. "Harry survived. He's coming."

The horses thundered into the clearing as Meade entered the tent. When Lucky swished back the tent flap he stiffly bowed low and announced, "Doctor. Your horse saddled and waiting."

Meade smiled broadly. "This is the best hunting camp I've ever been in. Steaming hot coffee served to me in my sleeping bag, breakfast at dawn, and the horses here for an early start. Lucky, you're my boy!"

Pleased but embarrassed by this praise, Lucky crossed his eyes, sucked in his lips, and idiotically whined "Uhhhh."

Copper, following Lucky like a shadow, poked his head into the tent, and Lucky gave him a biscuit. The two had become inseparable—two developing colts. Copper knocked over the sugar bowl and I yelled, "Lucky, get that horse out of the cook tent."

Ruth asked Harry, "Is Lucky joking about grizzly tracks?"

Harry, an Indian of few words, merely held up one finger. Meade assured us, "I saw the track on the lakeshore while I was fishing."

Ruth asked, "Do they come into tents?"

Lucky's dark eyes looked at Ruth. "Sure all time. They sleep in tents." She rolled her eyes, not knowing what to believe.

Breakfast over, I asked Harry, "Are you going to try for that ram up there," pointing to a rocky shelf high on a mountain four or five miles away. The sheep was a white pinpoint to the naked eye, but I had studied it with my 12 power binoculars for a long time, and I was convinced it was a lone ram.

Harry shook his head. "Hard stalk. Sheep got forty-power eyes. See us. We go up pass."

Ruth and I watched Harry and Meade ride their horses up a rocky trail until they were pinpoints in the distance. Then we gathered paints, brushes, and canvases and followed up the same trail until we reached the top of a knoll with a glorious view of the valley. The previous night we had given the valley the name *Neechemoos*, a Cree Indian word meaning "dear," because it was so dear to prospector Jack's heart.

The valley enchanted me with its haunting silence, yet life was everywhere. We watched the white ram work his way up to the ragged mountain skyline. A small bunch of caribou, white necks flashing in the sun, trotted down the winding creek. Four wild swans rested on the sapphire lake. Ptarmigan, already partly winter-white, cackled as they flew about. Unlike Jack, I thought they were expressing their joy at living in such a wondrous place.

Beyond the lake, wild, rugged, purple mountains loomed mysteriously in the distance, calling, calling, calling. Inside I ached with the beauty, the wildness, the freedom of *Neechemoos*.

That day Ruth painted Jack's big gnarled spruce tree and the full-headdressed Indian chief chiseled into a cliff by the elements. She shaped the painting with gobs of paint, so Jack could read it like Braille.

As we worked, far below, near camp, Lucky worked at building a stout saddle rack. He had such a high regard for Louis that all I had to say was, "Louis wanted this or that," and Lucky would industriously go to work. When done, he always asked, "Louie Brown. He like that?"

The sun had dropped behind a high mountain when we saw puffs of smoke from camp. Ruth sighed, "That's Lucky's signal for us to get back and start supper."

That evening Meade was as happy as I've ever seen a hunter/client, and he hadn't even fired a shot. At supper he chuckled, "Harry and I ran right into a sheep convention today. Or, maybe it was a sheep PTA meeting."

"Salt lick," Harry grunted.

"We counted forty-two ewes and lambs. What a sight! A regular sheep pasture."

Lucky snorted. "But Doctor, where ram?"

Meade smiled with confidence. "Oh, we'll bring a ram back tomorrow. Lucky, what kind of weather will we have tomorrow?"

Lucky stepped outside, looked around, wet a finger, tested the air. "Rain," he announced. "I hope you're wrong," Meade said.

Morning dawned bright and sunny. Harry and Meade rode up the trail toward the pass, taking a packhorse. They carried our art supplies as far as our favorite knoll, and later, when the sun had warmed the valley, Ruth and I climbed to paint. As we left camp, Lucky was teaching Copper things that every good pony should know.

Ruth shoved a canvas and a brush at me. "Paint that cow moose and her calf, there at the base of the mountain."

"You've overrated my ability. I'll paint the mountain. You'll have to paint the moose."

We painted blissfully for several hours. Ruth, with sure strokes, was painting the moose when Lucky arrived with Copper trotting behind.

Lucky leaned on Copper's neck and looked over Ruth's shoulder, watching her swift brush strokes. He burst out laughing. "That moose nose look funny."

"Shut up. You couldn't even paint a jackass," Ruth jabbed back.

Lucky snatched the brush from her hand, grabbed palette and paper, and leaped across the knoll with Copper scampering after him. With a yell, Ruth ran after him to retrieve her equipment. At the moment, high in the distant mountains, we heard a booming rifle shot.

It had to be Meade. "Do you think they got a grizzly?" Ruth asked.

Lucky laughed scornfully. "One shot? Maybe little mouse."

Ruth retrieved her brush and paints, and Lucky raced downhill, followed by an exuberant Copper.

We became so absorbed in painting that we were surprised to hear a shout and see Harry leading Dina, with an excited Meade on his horse, following behind. Huge sheep horns were tied onto Dina's saddle. We hurriedly followed the hunters down the trail.

By the time we arrived in camp, Harry had sheep ribs roasting over the campfire. Ruth set the table with a large bouquet of wild lupines, bluebells, arctic poppies, and ferns in a glass jar. She hung my painting on the tent wall. Lucky had covered the ground inside the tent with fresh spruce boughs, and the tent was filled with a sweet pungent fragrance. Intermingled with the odor of spruce, was the tantalizing cinnamon and nutmeg aroma of peach pie.

"Rib done," Harry called. Ruth and I went out to help carry in the tea and a pot of beans.

As we reentered the tent, Ruth let out a yell of rage. Her beautiful bouquet had been replaced by an old rusty tin can filled with dead weeds. In place of my painting, was Lucky's caricature of an old nag with me in the saddle. Ruth flourished a stick and started after Lucky. Laughing, he vaulted pack boxes and table. Horrified that this tomfoolery was upsetting the dignity of our hunting camp, I begged them to stop. When Ruth poured the tea, we were short a cup. When Lucky too feverishly joined the search for it, I became suspicious.

After the dishes were washed, Lucky, wearing a clean shirt, and with his hair slicked down, presented himself at the cook tent. With great dignity he announced, "Tonight we celebrate big sheep hunt. Show start pretty soon."

Lucky left with Dina, and returned soon with her pulling a large log. He went after another. Ruth sniffed, "He doesn't have a campfire in mind. I think he's going to start a forest fire."

Meade stuck his head through the tent flaps. "I have orders to tell you to hurry. The performance is about to begin. I have no idea what this tribute to my success is going to be, but with Lucky as master of ceremonies, I'll bet it won't be dull!"

When Ruth and I neared the campfire, Ruth shrieked, "Lucky John, you're a hypocrite."

Ignoring her, Lucky adjusted his tin-cup microphone, which was lashed to a stick, and cleared his throat.

"Doctor, you good hunter. Harry say you one-shot doctor. We congratulate you."

Motioning for us to join him, Lucky loudly clapped his hands. Meade solemnly rose, bowed stiffly in all directions, and sat down.

Lucky continued, "So tonight we have big powwow for good luck to mighty hunter."

With his opening speech ended, Lucky picked up his guitar. "I sure miss Louie Brown. He best guide in Yukon. I dedicate my first song to Big Boss."

As I heard the first bars to a song I well knew, I felt like choking. Through those dreadful days in the hospital when it had ground out of the creaky photograph, Louis had called it his song. Lucky's voice soared through the night.

"Oh what a beautiful morning
Oh what a beautiful day
Ah got a beautiful feeling . . . ."

I jumped to my feet. Ruth, sensing my feelings, hissed, "Lucky, shut up."

Lucky gave us a startled look, and without a pause swung into "I'm in the Jailhouse Now. I'm in the Jailhouse Now." His chaps flapped to the rhythm, and his hat wobbled to the back of his head. He looked through his fingers as if they were bars, and jabbed a thumb at Harry.

Harry grinned with embarrassment.

Lucky strode back to the tin-cup microphone. "This next number I dedicate to Martha, Harry Baum's girlfriend. Kneeling in front of Harry, our teenage wrangler soulfully lifted his voice.

"Martha, your eyes shine like two beer bottles

You hug like two grizzly bears

You got two legs like trees

You got two big . . . ."

Lucky collapsed with laughter and rolled on the ground. Harry was a red Indian now. At least his face was. He shrank deeper into the shadows.

Ruth jumped up and grabbed the guitar, went to the microphone and said, "Let's get on with the program." To my astonishment she started to play, and to all our delight, she sang a light merry tune, "Who Shot a Hole in My Sombrero?" Her voice was sweet and clear, with the richness of tone that captivated.

"Who put de bullet through de hat?

Who shot a hole in my sombrero?

Oh, who would do a thing like that?"

Each time Ruth sang, "Who shot a hole in my sombrero?" Lucky fell to the ground and poked his finger through his hat. Meade held his sides, roaring with laughter.

"Lucky, you're some boy!"

Lucky hopped up and adjusted his tin-cup microphone. "Mrs. Brown, I tell you no lie. This true story. Once my dad 'n me go hunt'n. Tie dog with chain to my belt. Lots stuff to carry.

"Pretty soon, Dad yell 'grizzly! Look out, him com'n.'

"Me t'row down everyt'ing and run like hell. Climb little spruce tree."

At that, Lucky started to climb a little spruce tree near the fire. When he was halfway up he shouted, "T'at bear com'n fast. T'at dog still hang'n on me. Grizzly growl, swat at dog. T'at dog run like hell. Come end of chain, pull me like hell, and . . . ."

Lucky had reached the tip of the little tree and it bent double under his weight, and the seat of his pants hit the ground.

Lucky yelled, "Bear him com'n' again." My wrangler started to climb the tree again.

Meade was trying to catch his breath as he heaved with mirth. "Lucky, I hope I don't have such a bad time with my grizzly."

I called to Lucky, "You'd better end your tale before you break your neck."

Meade agreed with me, and suggested, "Lucky, why don't you and Ruth sing a song."

Ruth and Lucky whispered together, and I heard her softly hum, teaching Lucky a tune. Lucky removed his cowboy hat and sat beside Ruth, his dark boyishness in sharp contrast to Ruth's blond hair and fair skin. Their voices rose in a haunting harmony.

"It was under northern skies

Violins and guitars

Played a dreamy waltz just for you

And as they softly played

Our hearts quietly strayed

Along with the Peace River Waltz."

Meade looked at me and smiled. Sparks from the fire drifted lazily up through the dark branches of old Jack's gnarled spruce, to disappear above in the soft glow of northern lights.

After another verse, the song ended, but there was no applause. We seemed to be gripped in the spell of *Neechemoos*.

Lucky stood again at his tin-cup microphone and seriously announced, "Next number. We have famous, powerful, great, medicine man. Harry Baum will perform the No-Rain-Dance."

"That's great," Meade smiled. "Harry and I are going grizzly hunting tomorrow and we don't want it to rain."

Lucky bowed low to Harry, who kneeled on his heels in the darkness. Even with Lucky's encouragement, I doubted that Harry would perform. Lucky brought out the tin dishpan and began a repetitious, rhythmic beat on it with two sticks. I was preparing to tell Lucky to go on with the program, when a blood-curdling yell shattered the quiet mountain air and Harry fiercely leaped into the firelight.

The sudden and violent action and shrill screech from Harry startled even Lucky, I think, for there was a momentary pause in his beating of the pan. Then, in a frenzy, Lucky brought the sticks down on the pan in a thunderous, wild, eerie pounding.

Harry bent low and with another primitive screech, he snatched a hatchet from a stump. Hatchet raised high, Harry vaulted across the flames of the campfire. The violence and primitive emotion released by the two Indians frightened me and I shrank back and tumbled backward off the log I sat on.

Without taking her hypnotized gaze from Harry, Ruth yanked me back beside her.

Fiendishly grimacing, and with savage war whoops, Harry sprang and leaped around the fire. Now he brandished the hatchet close to the ground. Next, he leaped with a blood-curdling yell, holding it high in a threatening gesture. He appeared as light as a feather as he leaped about the dim light of the flickering fire.

After a time, Lucky abruptly stopped pounding on the tin tom-tom, and Harry violently buried the hatchet in the stump from where he had snatched it. It was over. We, the audience of three whites, sat glued to our logs, amazed, frightened, awed.

Lucky, delighted with the audience reaction, led us in thunderous applause.

Meade shook himself and stood. "After that magnificent demonstration of weather control, I'm sure Harry and I will have a nice sunny grizzly hunt tomorrow. However, in keeping with custom, I again ask Lucky to give his weather report. How about it, Lucky?"

"Sunshine," Lucky promptly reported. "When Harry do the No-Rain-Dance, sun always shine."

Indian Tact

R uth sat up in our bed, pulling the down robe that covered both of us off of me. She sputtered, "What's that?"

"Lie down. You're letting in the cold air," I pleaded, half asleep. Ruth stood up, groaning, "It can't be. It just can't."

"What can't be?" I mumbled.

"Dolores, wake up. It's raining torrents. It's a cloudburst, and you're sleeping under a sieve."

Threshing soggily out of the sleeping bag I blinked unbelievingly. Rain poured through the open tent flap. "But Harry danced the No-Rain Dance."

Ruth snorted, "You didn't fall for that? It was more of a demon dance. I wouldn't be surprised if it rained, hailed, and snowed, with a tornado or two thrown in."

No wonder I had slept so uncomfortably. I was lying on squishy wet lumps of feathers.

Wind gusts snapped the slack tent canvas, sending showers of icy mist over our clothing and sleeping bag.

A burst of song exploded near.

"Mrs. Brown, I tell no lie, E-I-E-I-O

Grizzly get'n closer all the time, E-I-E-I-O"

"Lucky, we're drowning," I called. "Tighten those ropes. The tent is sagging."

Whistling cheerfully, Lucky snapped a rope tight and the tent flipped up, leaving a foot of air space between the bottom of the wall and the ground. Wind blasted icy rain on our bare feet.

"Lucky, build a fire in the cook stove, will you?" I asked.

Lucky smothered a laugh and answered me, "Uhhhhhh," a simple-minded whine he had picked up from someone in Keno.

Rain can ruin a big game hunt. I dreaded facing Meade that morning, but I had underestimated him. He came to breakfast beaming, and blithely remarked, "One has to expect some bad weather. Part of every hunt, you know."

Harry came in scowling so darkly that no one dared ask him what had gone wrong with his No-Rain Dance.

Meade smiled at Harry, "Well, Harry, guess we'd better not tackle bears today. It's a good time for me to do my washing."

"Plenty water," Lucky snickered.

"And Harry has to skin your sheep head and flesh the cape," I said, looking pointedly at Harry.

Harry grunted and left. Since our sleeping tent had no stove, Ruth and I had to dry our bedding and clothes in the cook tent. Neither Harry nor Lucky showed up for meals. While rain drummed on taut canvas tents, the valley echoed to the strumming of guitar and wheezing harmonica. Once Meade came in and reported that the two Indians weren't starving—they were boiling meat over their campfire.

Meade left, commenting, "Weather doesn't look too promising. Wonder if my washing will ever get dry?"

When he was gone I muttered to Ruth, "He'd better start wondering if his sheep head is ever going to get skinned."

Late in the day we heard the guitar and Lucky's voice.

"Mrs. Brown, I tell you no lie

Harry say he rather die

Than clean that bloody hide."

I stuck my head out of the tent. "This is no laughing matter. What is Louis going to say if that sheep cape isn't properly taken care of, and the hair slips?"

Lucky came into the tent, dripping, to get sugar for his and Harry's tea.

"Has Harry skinned that sheep head yet?"

"He go'n do it tomorrow, maybe next day."

I stamped my foot. "He's going to do it right now. NOW!"

Lucky dived under the table and peeked out. "Ruth, Mrs. Brown sure mad. I scared."

"You bet I'm mad."

"My dad say be happy all time."

I stalked out of the cook tent and marched down the trail. Halfway to the tent shared by Harry and Lucky, I was intercepted by Lucky.

"Mrs. Brown, talk first to Harry. How good he sings. Say, 'That harmonica play'n real thing.' Then say, 'Harry, how your girlfriend?'

"Then pretend just happen to see sheep hide. Say, 'Guess it don't matter hide rot, but too bad hunter not give you big tip to buy new gun.' "

I thanked Lucky for his coaching. I found Harry pouring his soul into his harmonica. I cleared my throat, and coughed. Harry continued playing, but not quite so loud.

"Harry," I said, "When do you think it'll stop raining?" I stopped, dismayed. The weather was not a good topic to discuss with Harry at the moment. I shouted, "You play beautifully."

If Harry was aware of my presence, he gave no sign. I had an inspiration. "Lucky is down in the cook tent picking out a gift from the catalog for his Mary. What kind of a gift do you want to give Martha?"

"Power saw," said Harry, looking interested.

"That's no gift for a girl. Go down and Ruth will help you pick out something Martha will like. Oh, for goodness sake. There's the sheep head. Mr. Ion will surely give you a big tip if you do a good job skinning and fleshing that cape." Then I fled.

Harry and Lucky spent the evening making their gift selections. Ruth talked with Harry, and he reluctantly relinquished the power saw for a turquoise-colored set of dishes for Martha. Lucky selected a phonograph for Mary. I was to mail the order when I flew back to Mayo at the end of Meade's hunt.

Rain still fell the next morning. Numerous waterfalls now splashed down the barren limestone cliffs on the eastern side of the lake. Ruth stood beside me watching the gay waterfalls merrily tinkle down from the dizzying heights to the lake.

The rain tapered off around midday. Lucky arrived from Meade's tent. "Doctor say too late to hunt bear. He want to hunt moose."

"Of course. Tell Harry."

"Harry say he don't want to go."

"That's ridiculous. He's the guide."

"Mrs. Brown. Lucky get Doctor moose. Hunt as good as Harry, me."

"No."

"Harry clean'n sheep hide. Take all afternoon."

I hesitated. If Harry at last was fleshing the sheep cape, I certainly didn't want to stop him.

"Lucky get Doctor one big moose today," Lucky pleaded.

"Very well. But for goodness sake, don't lose your hunter, get lost or . . . ."

"Oh, Mrs. Brown," Lucky laughed, "Better guide than Harry, me."

"You'll have to prove it."

Lucky left, singing happily.

"Mrs. Brown, I tell you no lie,

Get moose for Doctor, or die."

Ruth hitched a ride with Lucky and Meade, and set up her easel by a large boulder. She wanted to paint the waterfalls. She waved a red scarf to let me know she had arrived safely.

Parka squirrels (ground squirrels) were abundant near camp. They were cute, and we enjoyed their antics. However, they soon realized we meant them no harm. Within a few days of our arrival they started to raid the cook tent to steal dried fruit, rice, butter, and anything else we didn't put away.

I started to mix a batch of bread dough, but had to toss a white-chinned squirrel we had named Oscar out of the tent with threats of execution if he returned. Then I trotted to the nearby tent to check on Harry. His head was still bent over the sheep cape, so I didn't disturb him. I returned to my baking.

B-OO-OO-M-M. A rumble and a roar filled the valley. I ran out of the tent. A huge limestone crag high above the valley slowly crumbled and hurtled down the mountain in a growing avalanche of rocks and dirt. It was headed straight for the big boulder where Ruth was painting.

I screamed, "Harry. My God, Ruth's under that!"

Harry, staring from the door of his tent, yelled, "Mountain come down."

I ran up the trail to him, shouting, "Help me get Ruth out."

Harry slapped a saddle and bridle on Trigger. Leaping on, he pulled me up behind and we raced along the lakeshore. A few stray rocks were still bouncing down the steep slope, and once Trigger reared to dodge one of them. We reached the place where Ruth had been. Harry swung me off as he brought Trigger to a sliding stop.

He leaped from the saddle, looking up at the mountain warily, "Rain, he make mountain bad. Find Ruth quick. Get hell out. Maybe more rock fall."

"She was by that large boulder. Where was it?"

Harry leaped over the jumble of rocks, searching. I shouted, "Ruth. Ruth!"

There was no sign of the girl. Where the trail had been was now a jumble of rocks. Dust was still rising. After a time the dust cleared, and we found the big boulder Ruth had been near. It was half-buried in the slide.

"Ruth. Ruth!" Harry called.

We heard a muffled, choking sound. Harry started clawing at the rocks.

"Ruth!" I screamed. "Can you hear me?"

A tiny voice came from beneath the rocks. "I'm under here."

"Keep talking so we can find you," I shouted.

Side-by-side, Harry and I tugged, hauled, and threw rocks. We came to one we couldn't move.

Harry brought Trigger, and with a rope the powerful horse dragged the rock aside.

Now we could see Ruth's blue slacks wedged in a hole under the boulder. Harry crawled down, grabbed her arm, and slowly pulled her out.

"Are you hurt?" I cried, hugging her.

"I don't think so. If I hadn't dived in that hole fast I'd have been squashed," she said, shakily.

Harry hustled us away from the site. "Lots rain no good. Make mountain soft."

When we neared camp I suggested, "Let's all have some coffee. It'll settle our nerves."

Ruth entered the cook tent, and shrieked with laughter. I thought she was hysterical from her narrow escape, and dashed into the tent, with Harry right behind. We stood stunned.

The eight loaves of bread I had left to raise had flowed over the spruce bough floor like an advancing glacier. Cinnamon rolls I had hurriedly dropped on top of the stove when I had heard the slide and dashed off, now covered the lids of the stove. It was half burned. A dishpan of dough I had left on the table had flowed over the sides of the pan, and was spreading over most of the table. Stuck in the middle of this dough, like a centerpiece, was Oscar, the parka squirrel.

Harry loudly guffawed, pointing, "Good trap!"

Oscar raised one little paw, gooey with dough, and chittered at us. I grabbed him by the scruff of the neck so he couldn't bite, and held him while Ruth washed the dough from his feet. When he was clean, I let him go with a warning that next time he would get the axe.

What a mess it was. Harry was a good sport and helped us clean up. He lugged the old spruce bough carpet out, and replaced it with fresh evergreens. The stove was almost impossible to clean. Finally Harry gave it a good scraping with a horseshoe.

While I stirred another batch of dough, Harry went to the far end of the lake and left a note in the trail, warning Lucky and Meade of rock slides. "Return to camp on the west side of the lake," the note concluded.

Harry sat drinking tea long after supper that evening. He was listening for the sound of horses. Eight o'clock went by, then nine o'clock. No sign of the hunters. Nervously, I said, "If Lucky took Meade around by Norshaw Lakes, they won't get back in time for Meade to catch his plane."

Ruth, also worried, said, "I think they're lost. You had better send Harry to track them down."

Harry grinned. Suddenly, it occurred to me that Lucky, with his love of teasing, might be getting into Harry's hair. Harry gave every indication that nothing would please him more than to have to track down the lost wrangler.

When ten o'clock neared, Ruth said, "Dolores, stop pacing. You're wearing out the spruce bough carpet."

I stopped, my mind made up. "Harry, I guess it's up to you to rescue our hunter from whatever mess Lucky has got him into."

Harry showed a row of gleaming teeth. I said, "Get your packsack. I'll make sandwiches and tea for you, and for the survivors—if there are any."

Harry nodded, almost laughing. Shouldering his pack, he vanished into the black night. Ruth and I sat with cups of strong coffee, prepared for an all-night vigil. I gritted my teeth, "If Lucky . . . ."

"Sh-h-h," Ruth held up a hand for silence. Came a faint nicker. We bolted through the tent flaps. Again came a nicker from down the trail. It was Dina. A cheery voice rang out, "Hello, everyone."

Meade's voice didn't sound distressed. On the contrary, it had an excited lilt. He called, "Be with you as soon as we change our wet clothes."

Minutes later Meade entered the cook tent smiling. "Wow. Have we ever had a day. Wait until Lucky comes," as he gratefully accepted a cup of hot coffee.

Lucky arrived grinning, followed by a sour-looking Harry.

"Lucky, did you find a moose for Mr. Ion?" I asked.

Lucky gave me a scornful look, and then his eyes grew intense with excitement.

Meade couldn't contain himself any longer. "Lucky, tell them what happened today."

Lucky wasn't to be hurried. He looked at me with glowing eyes, "Mrs. Brown, you know that pass that turn to Wind River?"

I nodded. Lucky continued, "That place too far. About two o'clock we at little lake this side pass."

Meade fidgeted. He was anxious to get to the exciting part of the story, but Lucky, savoring every minute, took his time. "Watch by lake. Know moose there, me. Tell Doctor, 'Moose, he go'n get up three thirty.' "

Meade jabbed his finger at his wristwatch and chuckled, "That moose was right on time. Exactly at three thirty, a monster of a bull heaved himself up out of the brush and stood there for a long time. Then he walked down into the lake."

"Take Doctor close, closer, closer," Lucky continued.

Meade laughed with glee. "If I hadn't stopped Lucky, we would have had to bulldog him!"

Lucky said, "Tell Doctor, 'Shoot'm in the middle and . . . .' "

"I didn't understand what Lucky meant, so I shot him in the shoulder," Meade interrupted.

Lucky shook his head. "Big bull. Drop dead in deep water."

"That's why Lucky told me to shoot him in the middle—so he would get out of the lake before he dropped dead."

"Doctor know now. Wouldn't listen to Lucky. Lucky good guide. Know all 'bout moose."

Meade rocked happily on the pack box. "What a moose! What a set of antlers!"

"Sure. 'Bout ninety inches," Lucky bragged.

Harry gave a disgusted grunt and left. Meade looked admiringly at the teenage wrangler/guide, "Lucky worked for two hours in that ice cold water. He was up to his waist, but he got my moose out. He fastened a rope to the moose's legs. Then Dina, how she pulled! Lady helped. Together they got that moose out of the lake.

"But wait. I'm ahead of my story. After I shot the moose, Lucky had to walk back a couple of miles to get the horses. While he was gone, two big bull moose came along the hillside. Why, I could easily have shot both of them! They were huge!"

Lucky shook his head. "Your moose bigger."

"Yes. Mine is the biggest moose I've ever seen."

Our hunter was bubbling with joy. He said, "Now, if I can get a grizzly . . . ."

Harry arrived for some sugar as Lucky was promising, "Don't worry Doctor. Lucky find you grizzly. Tomorrow!"

A smoldering fire flashed from Harry's eyes. When we were alone, Ruth said, "My guess is there's a hot grizzly stew brewing, and it'll boil over in the morning."

Grizzly

R ain had washed *Neechemoos* clean. The dazzling sun rising above the high surrounding mountains intensified the autumn reds and yellows, turning the valley into a gorgeous multi-hued tapestry.

Meade drank a last cup of coffee while waiting for Lucky to bring in the horses. Through the open cook tent flap I watched Harry, sitting on a log, glassing the mountains. I wondered if it would settle the dispute if he and Lucky drew straws on who would guide Meade to a grizzly. Suddenly, Harry tensed. He had seen something. Turning, he caught Meade's attention and with a jerk of head motioned our hunter outside. Meade eagerly took the binoculars Harry handed him. He peered through the magnifying glasses for a long time. Then he and Harry conferred in low whispers. Next Meade dashed to his tent and came out with his rifle.

Harry appeared with his rifle, and together they took off on foot through the brush, headed up the slope west of the lake.

Ruth poked her head out. "What's up?"

"Maybe a grizzly," I answered.

Ruth threw down the dishtowel. "I'm going to see if I can spot it."

I followed her outside, but all I could find on the mountainside with my binoculars were two cow caribou. I handed Ruth the glasses and went back to finish the dishes. Ruth soon called, "It's a bear!"

"A grizzly?" I asked.

"Never saw one. I wouldn't know," she answered.

I reached for the glasses. "Halfway up the mountain, right under that slide," Ruth directed.

I refocused and shifted the glasses. A movement. Then my heart leaped. What a magnificent animal! In the brilliant sunshine his cream-colored back gleamed. His legs were chocolate brown. His big shoulder hump rolled as he bowleggedly walked about, apparently searching for a marmot. Ruth and I shivered with excitement. The two caribou cows I had seen jerked their heads up and stood staring. Then we saw Harry and Meade climbing a ravine. The grizzly was leisurely working his way down the mountainside.

Ruth gave a soft squeal. "They're going to meet head on."

"Don't be fooled," I warned. "There's more distance between them than you think."

We nervously took turns watching the stalk. Meade remained right on Harry's heels. The bear, unaware of the approaching hunters, stopped to dig for a root.

"Any minute now, and they'll shoot," Ruth stuttered.

Suddenly, behind us, came a loud cracking and snapping of brush, bells rang, and the horse herd thundered into the camp clearing on a dead run. Lucky, yelled ahead, "Someone help tie 'm."

Ruth groaned. "The bear has turned. He's starting to run. He heard Lucky yell! He's going to get away."

Lucky rode up on Dina and slid to the ground. Ruth whirled and with blazing eyes said, "You've just ruined the most beautiful bear stalk."

Lucky was stunned. "Where? How? Me?"

Then his sharp eyes caught sight of the fleeing bear. It was running toward the far end of the lake. Jerking off his jacket, he unbuckled his chaps and threw down his hat. Then he took off on a dead run, yelling, "Head 'm off, head 'm off!"

Ruth grabbed her .303. "The little fool has no rifle, and they'll meet at the other end of the lake." Then she took off after Lucky.

Knowing that Ruth's experience with a rifle was limited, I ran for my .270 and leaped down the trail behind them. We had one advantage over the bear; the trail on our side of the lake was mostly level, while the bear had to climb through several gullies.

We jumped creeks, leaped over rocks. Across the lake, the grizzly skimmed the buckbrush.

Ahead, Ruth flew swiftly after Lucky. When the grizzly topped the first gully, Lucky was even with it. Then Lucky reached the end of the lake. He was yelling loudly, trying to turn the bear back. Ruth caught up with him, and she yelled too. All to no avail. The bear beat them to the end of the lake by 50 yards, and it never slowed as it disappeared down the trail.

I dreaded having to face Meade. He was bound to be disappointed. But again I had underestimated his sportsmanship. He came into camp laughing. "Harry and I decided we would rather collect a caribou! While we were on the mountainside, we saw a big bunch of bulls way down the valley."

That afternoon Meade and Harry returned with a fine set of caribou antlers, and one hind quarter of caribou meat. "Bring other meat wit' horses tomorrow," Harry promised.

"Caribou steaks for breakfast, Ruth?" Meade requested.

"Of course. With fried potatoes," she promised.

Lucky unloaded the caribou quarter and asked me where to put it.

"On those pack boxes in front of the cook tent," I directed.

Ruth was up early, urging Lucky to hurry after the horses. After we had coffee, she went to cut caribou steaks. She burst back into the tent, "The caribou meat is gone!"

"What are you talking about?"

"The whole quarter of caribou is gone. It was right there on those boxes," she wailed.

"Oh, Ruth, it's just another of Lucky's pranks," I soothed. "Ignore it. Don't say a word. Just cut some moose steaks."

At breakfast Meade commented, "I was anxious to see what caribou tasted like. Funny, but I can't tell the difference between this and moose."

Ruth didn't say a word. She looked accusingly at Lucky, who looked innocent, and continued to eat.

It was a glorious morning, and the crisp air was stimulating. All of us wanted to get out and do something. We decided that everybody would accompany Harry and the horses to retrieve the caribou meat. "Maybe bear find meat," Harry warned.

Harry and Meade went ahead, and Ruth and I followed when Lucky had saddled the packhorses. Harry and Lucky had decided to dry caribou and moose meat from the hunt, to pack out at the close of the hunt.

"Go 'head. Me catch up," Lucky told Ruth and me.

We rode down the lake, enjoying the day. Copper, full of the devil, scampered up and down the line of horses. The slick, fat horses gleamed in the morning light. I thought how different they appeared from the bony, long-haired apparitions they had been during their fearful struggle to survive the previous winter.

Queen and Trigger suddenly stopped, craned their necks, snorted, and ran off. Bunny jumped, landing stiff-legged. She was getting ready to give me the heave-ho to lighten her load for a quick getaway if the thing she was watching grew dangerous.

Following her wild-eyed stare, I saw a bobbing pair of caribou antlers showing just above the rim of a deep wash. Never had I seen caribou antlers perform such erratic movements. Neither had the horses, and Big Dan took off up a side creek at top speed. What in the world was going on? Was the caribou being killed by a bear? It looked like a death struggle, sure. But then, why was Copper trotting along right behind those antlers?

Ruth called, "There's something fishy about that caribou. I'm riding over to take a look."

I held my rifle across the saddle, ready, and followed. Ruth reached the rim of the wash, when, suddenly, the erratic caribou antlers lunged toward her. Baldy reared, and Ruth flew from the saddle. The antlers topped the edge of the ravine, and I caught a flash of blue jeans.

"Lucky," I yelled. "Get out from under those antlers."

Lucky howled with mirth. Then he climbed on his horse and deliberately fell off several ways to demonstrate to Ruth how funny she had looked when Baldy had bucked her off.

Clenching her teeth, Ruth broke off a long willow switch and climbed back on Baldy, determination in every move. Unaware, and sitting crosslegged on his horse, Lucky improvised.

"An old maid named Ruth

'Bout sixty years old, that's truth

From saddle she tried to fly

But all she . . . ."

Lucky heard pounding hoofs behind him. One look and he pulled his hat down with a yell, then spurred his horse into a dead run. Ruth, holding the willow switch over her head, was but one jump behind him.

Whooping with laughter and joy, Lucky leaped his horse across creeks, and jumped logs, but he couldn't lose the determined Ruth. I groaned. If they didn't break a horse's leg, they were certain to break their necks. Then a thought came; what if a grizzly was feeding on the caribou kill, and in their tomfoolery these two spoiled another stalk?

I spurred Bunny after the racing Lucky and Ruth. Bunny, excited, took the bit in her teeth, and all I could do was hang on until she decided to stop. I passed Meade and Harry in a blur. Lucky had pulled in his horse, and was circling back, with Ruth about a length behind. I managed to persuade Bunny to stop. Harry and Meade galloped up. Ruth and Lucky bore down on us. Harry held up a hand in warning, pointing ahead to where the caribou carcass lay, over a rise ahead.

Lucky dodged behind me, pleading, "Mrs. Brown, save me from that mean lady."

"Stop this nonsense and go round up the packhorses," I ordered.

We slowly rode behind Harry. He motioned, and we tied the horses and crawled to the rim of the rise, peeking over with binoculars. After a time, Harry grunted, "He gone."

I thought he meant the caribou, but he really meant that a bear had been there and had left. When we reached what was left of the carcass, we found that a bear had eaten a large chunk out of it.

Lucky arrived with the pack horses, and he and Harry loaded what was left of the meat onto packsaddles, and we rode back to camp in silence.

Meade wanted to leave at daylight next morning to climb across the pass to look for a grizzly. Lucky begged, "Mrs. Brown, get grizzly for Doctor, me. Like moose."

"You've lost Big Dan. Since you're the wrangler of this outfit, you're going to have to find him. Remember, you're the one who spooked him."

As Meade and Harry left camp, Ruth tossed a horseshoe after them for luck. Meade laughed, "I promise. I'll bring that grizzly back tonight."

By noon, black clouds rolled up over the limestone cliffs. Then came a deafening crash of thunder, followed by a blinding flash of lightning. In the distance, wind roared like a train speeding through the pass. The tents snapped and popped, and tarps blew from pack boxes, saddles, and blankets.

Ruth and I rushed about, tying loose items down. The mountains were hidden behind a dark curtain of rain. More thunder echoed among the crags, and rain fell in torrents.

Late in the day a drenched Lucky returned, leading Dan. After supper, I made chocolate fudge. While waiting for the hunters to return, we sat munching candy and rereading almost-worn-out funny books. Our last candle dimly lit the tent. We were low on sugar and salt. Our flashlight batteries had long ago expired.

"I'm afraid Meade won't get his grizzly. He has only two hunting days left," I commented.

Lucky nodded. "More better send Lucky for bear."

Ruth snorted. "Lucky, you sure don't lack for . . . ."

"Horse," Lucky said, holding up his hand for silence. Tense and alert, he jumped up and held back the tent flap.

Ruth and I stood beside him, straining our ears. Finally, we heard the dull clunk of a horseshoe hitting a rock. We rushed out.

Through the darkness came Meade's voice, "Harry got lost."

Then came Harry's voice. "Miss trail." He sounded rather happy over being lost.

Lucky whispered. "They not get lost. Somet'ing happen."

Meade rode into the faint light that came from the tent. "Give us a few minutes to change. We're both wet."

Minutes later, Harry and Meade arrived in the cook tent. Both looked exhausted. Meade dipped into his split pea soup, then dropped his spoon. He had to tell his story, no matter how hungry he was.

"Harry's never been lost," I commented.

"Aw, Harry didn't get lost. I was fooling."

Lucky giggled. "Harry looks like mouse swallow cat."

Harry did look self-satisfied. In the dim light, his face looked lean and hard. His dark eyes drooped with weariness. He appeared to have been through a strain.

Meade was a combination of smugness, happiness, and disbelief. Finally, he said, "Three grizzlies charged us!"

My jaw dropped. Lucky whistled. Ruth took Meade's half-eaten bowl of soup away from him, and sat impatiently.

"Tell us," Ruth begged. She made it clear she wasn't going to serve his supper until he told the story.

Meade continued, "Harry and I are lucky to be alive."

We all sat in silence as he detailed the exciting day.

"Harry and I rode through the pass. We were way past the sheep meadow when rain caught us. Soon we were soaked. We stopped and built a fire and got partly dried. We considered returning to camp, but Harry decided that the sky was clearing, so we went on.

"We stopped now and then to glass. Finally Harry held up three fingers and got out the spotting scope.

"I asked, 'Caribou?'

" 'Grizzly,' Harry answered. Believe me, my blood pressure shot up. We sat and Harry studied them for a long time through the scope. Then I looked. What a sight! One was a big silvertip, and the other two were darker, and nearly as large.

"Finally, Harry tested the wind, and made up his mind. 'Come,' he said.

"We tied the horses and stalked the bears. Harry went straight up the mountain, and I stuck with him. It was steep, tough climbing, but we kept going.

"Halfway to the bears, still above us, Harry rested. After watching me try to catch my breath, he decided we'd better wait until the bears worked down closer to us, giving me a chance to rest. He didn't want me to be panting when I shot.

"We crouched in a gully and watched as the bears moseyed here and there, moving closer and closer to us. Finally, Harry said 'Shoot.' I aimed and fired at the big silvertip. He dropped. Then, quicker than I could think, he was up. Then he charged us! The two other bears were right behind him. All three roared and popped their teeth as they ran right at us.

" 'Shoot. Shoot,' Harry yelled. I hesitated, knowing that my license allowed only one grizzly, but Harry yelled again, 'Shoot.' By the tone of his voice, I knew we were really in trouble, so I shot. When it was all over the silvertip was down, and a second bear was hard-hit. He took off up a ravine.

"I deliberately shot over the third bear, and he ran off into a jumble of boulders. It was near dark, and we couldn't see to track the wounded bear. We skinned the silvertip, and came home."

Meade stopped talking for a moment, as all of us stared at the two hunters. Then Meade said, "This was the most exciting day of my life. Those three bears were so close that I couldn't miss. I felt justified in shooting the second bear because our lives were threatened."

I looked at Harry. His black eyes were somber. He nodded to confirm Meade's story. He knew the consequence of allowing a hunter to shoot more than his limit. It's a sure way to lose a guiding license.

My mind whirled. Had Meade become overwrought and too frightened to think straight? I looked into his drawn face, and again into Harry's

Indian mask. It was clear that they had had a narrow escape, and that Meade had truly believed he had to shoot to save their lives.

They finished eating and headed for their tents and bed. Ruth groaned, "Yesterday we were worried because Meade didn't have a grizzly. Now we're worried because he has too many!"

"Ruth, what if Harry can't track that wounded bear? I don't want some poor prospector or trapper to die from an attack of that wounded grizzly. That has happened many times here in the Yukon."

The tent began to quiver. As usual, it was Dina, scratching herself on the tent ropes. She never went out to graze with the other horses, but preferred to stay near camp. I stood petting her and wishing that Louis was here. He was one hunter who would and could stay on that wounded grizzly's trail until he found him.

For Courage

At daylight both Meade and Harry still showed the strain of the grizzly charge. They also worried about the wounded bear, for they realized the great danger of tracking down that animal. Many northern hunters have been mauled or killed while trailing wounded grizzlies.

"Stay 'n' flesh silvertip hide," Harry suggested. He appeared reluctant to track down the wounded bear. Meade, on the other hand, was anxious to get started. "Harry and I will work it out, Dolores," he suggested.

After breakfast the two talked, and walked back and forth between their tents. Then, suddenly, they were on their way. It was clear that Harry wasn't going to burn the wind getting there. I asked Lucky, "What's wrong with Harry? Is he scared of that bear?"

Lucky grinned, "Harry say that bear different kind bear. That one go'n over mountain, bring back lots bears. They go'n tear Harry to pieces."

With that reassuring comment, Lucky wandered off to work with the horses and their tack. Ruth and I tried baking, but we burned a cake and a batch of cookies, and gave up. We simply sat watching the pass for the return of the hunters. To say that I was worried is an understatement.

As the late afternoon sun sank below the mountaintops, I decided I had made a mistake in allowing Meade to accompany Harry on such a dangerous errand. I should have sent Lucky with Harry instead.

As the evening shadows crawled across the valley Lucky stood by the cook tent. "Mrs. Brown. Look bad. One time in Alaska grizzly bite whole top man head. 'Nother time, he take man's eye out and . . . ."

"Lucky, will you please shut up," I snapped, nervously.

"But Mrs. Brown . . . ."

"Keep still."

"But Mrs. Brown. The hunters com'n."

"What! Where?"

The men rode wearily into camp. Harry flung a bloody sack containing the grizzly hide at my feet. Meade tiredly said, "Harry sure tracked that bear as if he were walking on eggs."

Next day was the last of Meade's hunt. We wanted to make it memorable. Harry and Lucky roasted moose ribs over a campfire. Ruth fixed Meade's favorite Franconia potatoes, while I made the last peach pie I would probably ever make for Meade.

We were all melancholy. Even the sun hid behind dark clouds from time to time. We posed Meade with his trophies and took many pictures.

Harry and Lucky arrived at supper dressed in new frontier slacks and embroidered gabardine western shirts. Meade wore a new bright plaid shirt, and his face was shiny after a fresh shave. We halfheartedly laughed at the moose ribs that hung 14 inches beyond the edges of our large graniteware dinner plates. Harry and Lucky attacked their ribs with hunting knives, while Meade, Ruth and I tackled ours in more conventional knife-and-fork style.

"I'd sure like to be able to stay and maybe hunt for a wolf," Meade said.

"I'd like to stay and do more sketching," said Ruth, sadly.

I loved the valley, and knew I would miss it, but I was anxious to see Louis.

Harry and Lucky were in high spirits. They would soon hear from their girlfriends, and Lucky was happy that his father was due to arrive to guide the next hunt.

Lucky insisted we have a last campfire show for Meade. We went through the motions, but the spontaneity was missing. Harry draped the silvertip grizzly hide over his shoulders and did a dance of a bear digging for marmots. Ruth and Lucky sang several songs. The program ended with Lucky singing a song he wrote for the occasion: "When I get sick and ready to die, I'll hire Harry to cry." Meade's laughter lacked the merry ring of other times.

Before I went to bed I gave Dina her usual goodnight petting and a lump of sugar. I lay for a long time staring at the stars through a gap in the tent. I longed to see Louis, but I dreaded leaving this valley to return to civilization. Admittedly, there were those who wouldn't consider the tiny towns of the Yukon civilization, but that is all I had known now for three years. How strange that I should both love and loath these small northern towns. In winter they were picturesque, with spirals of smoke rising above the snowy roofs. At other times they seemed to be the graveyard of all human virtues. I remembered a thought from Joseph Wood Krutch: "Joy has its roots in something from which civilization tends to cut us off."

Gradually sleep claimed me.

I awoke to the scream of a horse just outside the tent. Then came a deep growl. A wild snort from the horse followed. I knew it had to be Dina. Ruth and I leaped up, both of us yelling, "Harry! Lucky! Meade!"

Meade's voice soared reassuringly through the night air. "I'm coming."

A flashlight came wavering across the clearing, and Meade appeared in his underwear topped by his raincoat. He carried his rifle. "Are you girls all right?"

"Yes. But something is trying to kill Dina."

"I'll have a look around."

Ruth and I dressed and anxiously watched Meade's flashlight flick over the bushes. Another flashlight appeared, as Harry and Lucky ran down the trail.

"What you hear?" Lucky demanded. Shaking with cold and fright, Ruth answered, "Something was after Dina."

"What else you hear?"

"I heard a growl and a thump, thump," I said.

Harry nodded. "Bear," he proclaimed.

Rifles at the ready, they joined Meade in the search. Harry found Dina and led her to our tent. She was shivering with fright as he tied her close. Lucky brought the dishpan and an iron spoon. "You hear noise again, hit pan hard. My dad say t'at scare bear."

Neither Ruth nor I slept for the rest of the night. Suddenly we were both glad we were going home.

A rosy dawn lit the valley. I built a fire in the cook stove and we drank several cups of coffee. Ruth said, "You know, Meade deserves a medal. He was the first to come to our rescue."

"You're right! Let's have some fun, and make him one. We'll pin it on him just like King George pinned the medal on Mrs. Reynolds."

With the can opener Ruth removed the bottom of a shiny tin can, and punched a hole in the edge. Through the hole I threaded one of my red hair ribbons. With lipstick Ruth wrote, "For Courage."

At breakfast Ruth asked Meade to stand. Surprised and laughing, he stood while Ruth pinned on the medal with a large safety pin. I read the citation:

"In the face of danger, and under the most
terrifying conditions, while ferocious
beasts roamed boldly under northern
lights, Meade Ion of Grosse Pointe,
Michigan, answered a call of distress. With
complete disregard for his own safety, he
routed marauding bears. With deep
appreciation and gratitude this medal is
hereby bestowed in behalf of the
defended.

Miss Ruth Krebs

Mrs. Louis J. Brown

Dina"

Meade chuckled, "Thank you. I shall always keep this as a reminder of the wonderful times I have had on this hunt." Lucky jumped to his feet, "Doctor, you one hunter we never forget."

Later, Meade showed us the bear's calling card on the ground in front of his tent. "Girls, it's time you left. This is getting too close."

Ruth finished packing our duffel bags while I listed items needed for the next hunt. Remembering we were out of sugar, milk, and candles, I included them in the list. Lucky came in, "Mrs. Brown, don't forget caulk horseshoes. Get'm cold now. Go'n home, trail have lots ice. Need caulk, bad."

Caulked horseshoes have a tapered piece that project downward, giving a horse better footing on ice. Regular horseshoes are flat and they slip on ice.

"Louis told me he would send them. How about some heavy wool socks and shirts for you and Harry?" Lucky nodded, and handed me letters to his Mary, and Harry's Martha.

"You not forget phonograph for Mary?"

"Of course not."

While waiting for Pat Callison to arrive with his floatplane, Ruth and I took a short ride down the valley to say good-bye to our horses, Bunny and Bobo. The valley had never looked so beautiful. Ruth dabbed at her eyes. "I'll miss it all my life."

"PLANE!" Harry yelled. In the distance we heard the throb of an engine. Ruth and I raced back to camp. We stood on the shore and watched Pat make his usual flawless landing. Meade turned to Ruth and me. "I'm taking you, Ruth, and Louis to dinner tonight." Lucky said, "Doctor, don't forget to tell Louie his wrangler get you big moose."

Meade nodded. "I'll tell him, Lucky. And, Dolores, if an airplane crashes with me on the way home, there will be no regrets. On this hunt, I lived the dream of my life."

Engine idling, Pat's plane neared shore, and then the propeller quit turning. Lucky and Harry turned the plane and pulled the rear of the floats onto the beach. Pat opened the door and yelled, "Hurry. I have to make another trip with your hunter's baggage before dark."

Two hunters tumbled out and I hurriedly shook hands, a virtual "Hello. Good-bye."

I called, "Pat, aren't you bringing in two more men?"

"Not that I know of. Louis didn't say. Just another load of duffel."

Our bush pilot's haste confused me. "Pat, where's the mail?"

He tossed me a canvas sack. I tore into it. Fumbling through letters, I tossed mail to Harry and Lucky. At the bottom was a letter from Louis. I ripped open the envelope and started to read.

"You can read that on the way in. I've got to get back here with that load before dark. I have other trips tomorrow."

Ruth and I scuttled into the plane and Pat slammed the door behind us. I turned to wave. Lucky looked up from reading his letter with an expression of stark calamity.

Pat started the engine and pulled us offshore, then opened the throttle to send the plane skimming across the water.

Ruth yelled, "Lucky is trying to be funny. He's waving us back."

The plane lifted and roared over the tents. We cleared the pass and I read Louis' letter with growing horror. I screamed, "Pat, Pat, I've got to go back to the camp."

"What's the matter?" he yelled.

"I have to stay there for the next hunt."

Ruth grabbed my arm. "If you are staying, I am too."

"But Ruth, remember, bears are raiding camp."

"Two guns are better than one," she answered, stoutly.

Pat banked the plane and landed again on the lake and taxied to our camp. While he was taxiing, I shoved the outgoing mail into Meade's hands. "Please give this shopping list to either Louis or the store clerk. We need these supplies badly. Tell Louis to send Ruth and me some wool underwear and sweaters and . . . ."

Pat called back over his shoulder, "You'll need parkas. It's going to be cold. Some of the smaller lakes are already icing up."

Ruth handed Meade a painting of *Neechemoos* to give to old Jack.

Lucky and Harry turned the plane and pulled the rear of the floats onto the beach. I held out my hand, "Good-bye, Meade. You'll always be our favorite hunter."

He responded with emotion, "I'm coming back as soon as Louis has recovered and is hunting again."

Ruth and I jumped out of the plane. "Lucky, Louis wrote that your dad didn't come, and neither did the other man. Everyone else is off fighting forest fires."

Lucky gave me a sick grin. "Louie tell me too. Me, I so scare when you gone. T'at mean Lucky cook, Lucky wash dishes, Lucky guide, Lucky wrangle horses, Lucky do everyt'ing. Now you back Mrs. Brown. You be wrangler."

"Wrangler! Me? But I've got a Chief Guide's License!"

Lucky threw back his head and laughed. "Oh, but Mrs. Brown, Lucky have to guide."

Pat yelled, "I'll be back as soon as I can." He then restarted the engine and taxied out for takeoff.

The two hunters were E. J. Miller and Dr. Jardine, both from Michigan.

Miller was amused at the quick change of Ruth and my plans. "I'm glad we didn't lose our cook," he said.

Dr. Jardine called to Lucky, "Here, boy, carry these two suitcases up to camp. Let's get started hunting."

I was chatting with Miller when I looked up and cringed. Lucky, following Dr. Jardine up the trail, carried the two suitcases as though they were both full of lead: he clumped up the trail with his legs bowed out, in an exaggerated waddle. I looked to the heavens. What if the doctor turned and saw him?

Harry took Miller to camp. As he passed I called, "You and Lucky come back. We have something important to decide."

When the four of us—Harry, Lucky, Ruth, and I—were together, I explained. "Louis says winter is coming early. He doesn't think we'll be able to fly the hunters out from *Neechemoos*. It's a small lake, and it'll be one of the first to ice over. He thinks we should take them over to Three River Lake."

Harry spoke. "When hunt over, maybe that lake ice too."

"I suppose that's a chance we'll have to take."

Harry shook his head, frowning. "More long way."

Lucky ran for the map he and Harry had followed to reach *Neechemoos*. Three Rivers Lake was about 15 miles farther out in the bush. Ruth said, "That means if we get there and that lake is frozen too, and Pat can't land, it will be a 30-mile ride for nothing."

"That's the chance we'd have to take," I said. I sounded like a broken phonograph.

"And I suppose you'd have to pay the airplane charter just the same?" Ruth asked.

"That's right."

Lucky stood, head bent, seriously thinking—something he seldom did. Then he spoke, "Mrs. Brown, all ride out. Better."

Harry nodded. "Hunt here four, five day. Then go. Hunt all way back."

"It's going to be harder to make the trip back with the hunters," I predicted.

Harry agreed. "Three day from Keno, trail plenty bad. Muskeg, lotsa swamp."

Louis never took his hunters over such a trail, and I hesitated. Ruth exclaimed, "We have no choice. Look at the snow creeping down the mountains. And this lake is already icing around the edges."

Harry and Lucky went to retrieve the horses. Ruth started supper. In anticipation of soon getting sugar, I walked to a knoll and gathered blueberries for a pie.

My pail was full when I heard the hum of Pat's plane. How could he have made the trip so quickly? I reached the lake as Harry and Lucky arrived with the packhorses. Pat and his mechanic had most of the load on the beach by the time we arrived.

I stared. There were only four small boxes for us. The balance was a huge pile of the hunters' duffel. Pat climbed into his plane, calling back, "I'll see you at Three Rivers Lake in 20 days."

"Pat," I yelled. "No. We're all riding out."

"This is my last trip for you then?"

"Yes."

"So long then. And good luck."

We watched as he roared across the lake and lifted into the sky, heading for the pass. Lucky opened one of the boxes and held up a horseshoe. "Mrs. Brown. This no good."

There were no caulked horseshoes. I knew we would need them for steep, icy trails on our return home. Harry and I opened the other three boxes. There was no sugar, no candles, no warm clothing for Ruth and me. We stood and blankly looked at each other. What had happened? Either Pat hadn't waited for the orders to be filled, or Meade had forgotten. Perhaps the stores were out of everything we had ordered. We turned and watched our last link with civilization climb higher and higher until the plane became a speck, and then disappeared through the pass.

Bear Trouble

"**H**ard hunt, this'n," Harry grunted. He was referring to our short supplies.

"Don't let the hunters know," I admonished.

Lucky asked, "How you keep from hunter no candles, no sugar?"

Harry frowned. "Old time Indian, he have no candle, no sugar. He OK. He happy."

"Harry, you're a wise Indian," I said, feeling grateful there would be no complaint from him.

"We gonna head for jam," Lucky said.

I wondered if he meant we were headed for disaster. He laughed. "Know 'bout lots jam. In Keno, old prospector tell me he cache two cases jam in Moose Meadows."

Harry grinned. "Get hunter sheep, grizzly, everything damn fast. Then we go find jam."

Knowing the Indians' love for sugar and sweets, I was willing to bet they'd find it.

Ruth served a delicious supper; Moose Scalopini Marsala, Russian beets, macaroni and cheese, lime jello salad, and hot yeast rolls. The macaroni and cheese made such a hit with Mr. Miller that he even ate it for dessert.

While we were eating, Miller told me, "Your husband has a new cast, just to his knee. This makes it a lot easier for him to get around. He won't be able to bear weight on his foot for another two weeks. In about a month the doctor will remove the steel pin from his arm."

"Is his arm paining him?" I asked.

Dr. Jardine assured me, "Louie is doing fine."

I tried to keep my mind on the conversation, but I kept wondering how we were going to get through the hunt. I was grateful when Mr. Miller stood up and graciously thanked Ruth for the delicious supper.

A few moments later, with dignity, Lucky rose and said, "Thank you Ruth, for de-lish-shus supper."

Ruth looked at him in astonishment. She had been feeding him for more than 20 days, and this was the first time he had acknowledged his appreciation. We were amused to see how quickly Lucky imitated Mr. Miller.

Mr. Miller asked, "Ruth, how about frying some fish for breakfast?"

"Glad to, if I had any to fry."

"We'll take care of that right away."

"Harry, Lucky, are you going fishing with us?" Dr. Jardine asked.

Harry and Lucky were anxious to read their mail again. Both thought it beneath their dignity as big game hunters to waste time on little fish.

"Show Dr. Jardine and Mr. Miller the best place to fish, then come back," I suggested.

Disgusted because the fish weren't biting, the hunters soon returned. Harry and Lucky shared the last candle. We shared oranges, peaches, and candy which Louis had sent, and sat reading our mail with peach juice dripping down our chins. "We'll never be separated again," Louis had written me. He said that every time he heard a car he feared it was someone coming to tell him we were in trouble. He told me of a Whitehorse outfitter whose four hunters had bagged one sheep, one bear, one moose, and one caribou. Heck, we had collected that many trophies for just one hunter!

Lucky giggled and snickered happily over his Mary's letter. Ruth winked, "Dolores, do you smell orange blossoms?"

Lucky glanced up, "Mary say we be married soon as get back."

"Congratulations, Lucky," I offered.

"Mrs. Brown, what you give for wedding present?"

"Why, I don't know yet."

"Make it som'thin' big," he advised.

"That depends on whether you do a good job for me," I warned. "Now let's plan this hunt."

Harry shook head. "Hunter want bear, bad."

Ruth groaned, "Why does it always have to be a bear? I suppose it proves they have hair on their chest if they get one."

Harry rolled a cigarette, and commented, "Hunter have lots bags."

Lucky snorted, "Take big truck, haul all that stuff."

It was true that the two hunters had an unusual amount of baggage, and that some of the suitcases would be hard to pack on the horses. After discussion, we decided that the men would take a side trip while Ruth and I remained in camp. This would allow the hunters use of their things for a longer period. Once on the trail, it would be too much work to unpack all their duffel every night.

Harry stood. "Tomorrow take hunters, me. Lucky stay, cut camp wood. Next day we go on trip."

"That's fine," I agreed. "While you're gone with the hunters tomorrow, Ruth and I will bake and cook and get ready for your side trip."

As Harry and Lucky started to leave, Lucky said, "Well, Mrs. Brown, you wrangler now. Five o'clock in morning get up."

"Wrangler! Me?"

"Sure. Lucky guide now."

"OK. Where do I find them?" I asked, resigned.

Ruth spoke up. "Lucky, in the morning show me where the horses graze at night."

Lucky grinned. "OK Ruth. Be up early."

"I'll probably be yelling my head off trying to get you up," Ruth retorted.

When I awoke, Ruth and Lucky were both gone, and I hurried to cook breakfast for Harry and the two hunters. I wanted them to be ready to leave as soon as the horses reached camp.

The previous night they had ordered steaks for breakfast, but when I went to the tree where we had cached the meat, none was left. I decided to give Lucky a piece of my mind. His inventive pranks were becoming less and less funny.

Eight o'clock came, then nine, and ten. The hunters paced in front of their tent. By eleven o'clock I was furious. Did Lucky and Ruth think the hunters were each paying $55 a day to sit in camp? Finally, at 11:30 the horses pounded down the trail, driven by Lucky and Ruth, who were almost exploding with excitement.

They pulled fish out of their boots, from their pockets, even from under their shirts. When Lucky removed his hat a couple of fish tumbled out. Breathlessly, Ruth explained, "Dolores, we came to this creek and it was black with grayling. The hunters didn't catch any fish for me to fry for breakfast, so we jumped in and caught bucketsful with our hands!"

She looked at the hunters, expecting praise. The hunters returned her look with cold, steely eyes. Later I had to explain that our clients preferred to shoot their own bears and catch their own fish. In fact, that's what they were paying for.

Harry left with the hunters. Ruth helped Lucky with the crosscut saw, while I melted moose tallow, pouring it into tin cans with string wicks. I hoped they would make usable candles. As I worked, I heard Ruth and Lucky arguing, and dashed out in time to see Ruth gripping tightly one end of a red blanket. Lucky pulled on the other end, shouting, "You not take this from my horses."

"To blazes with your old horses," Ruth yelled.

"Stop it," I screeched. "Do you want to tear a perfectly good four-star trapper's blanket to pieces?"

"That's what I told him," Ruth grated. "Dolores, we need this to make some warm shirts for us."

Lucky yelped, "Your tent on fire!"

"Don't play that trick on me. I'm not letting go."

Smoke poured from the cook tent, and I ran to put out the moose tallow fire. Ruth came in grumbling, "He's hid all the good horse blankets. We're going to freeze if we can't find something warmer to wear."

"Never mind. Tomorrow when they're gone maybe we can find where he cached them.

The hunters returned late in the day. Harry swung down from his saddle all grins. He strutted to the saddle rack and hung up the hide of a huge wolf. He was proud of his hunter. "Kill 'm one shot."

Miller had reason to be happy. The wolf was an unusual light color, almost white. Further, a wolf is a trophy rarely collected by sport hunters.

After supper that night, Lucky arrived in the cook tent and announced, "Maybe not go on side trip, me."

"Of course you're going. Everything is ready."

"'Fraid leave you two alone. Might shoot each ot'er."

"You think of the stupidist things," Ruth snorted.

Lucky shook his head. "Don't stand behind when you have gun. Don't carry shell in barrel. Want you bot' alive when come back."

"I appreciate your concern, Lucky, but your worries are needless."

"Not scare stay alone?" Lucky asked.

"Of course not," Ruth shouted. "Dolores is a crack shot, and I'll back her up!"

Lucky gave us a crooked smile and left. Next morning he and Harry hurriedly saddled up while the hunters scuttled back and forth between their tent and the packhorses. Finally, Harry and Lucky had to add another packhorse. As they rode off, Lucky turned in his saddle to remind me, "You have five horses. Don't lose any. Need all to go home."

We watched until they disappeared on the far end of the lake. We sighed, looked at each other, and burst into laughter. We were alone at last in our valley. No meals to cook for hunters, or Harry and Lucky. We had only five horses and ourselves to look after. We could truly relax for the first time in weeks.

In the early afternoon we decided to take a swim in the lake. Since the lakes at the elevation of *Neechemoos* do not thaw until July, and they start to freeze over in September, we weren't planning on a long leisurely dip. We gingerly toed the shore ice, and decided the only way was to dive in. We sputtered to the surface, gasping with shock from the icy water. Ruth stumbled ashore, "I almost had a heart attack!"

We dashed back to camp and checked the horses. We decided we would turn them loose late in the day. That way they would be hungry enough to stay in the meadow where they grazed until morning.

With chattering teeth we crawled into our sleeping bag to get warm, and promptly fell asleep. Next thing I knew Ruth was shaking me awake. She whispered, "What's that sound. Something big is out there. I can hear it breathing!"

I sat up listened. The sound frightened me. It wasn't a horse.

Then a parka squirrel screeched his alarm call, and the horses wildly snorted. "Ruth, get your rifle," I whispered.

I grabbed my .270 and crawled under the tent wall. Then I slowly stood up. When I turned to look I almost jumped out of my socks. There, a few feet away, stood the largest black bear I had ever seen.

"Shoot!" screamed Ruth, from behind me.

At the sound of Ruth's voice, the bear whirled. I fired a quick shot at it, then drew back the bolt to slam in another shell. The bolt stuck. The bear, frightened by the sound of the shot, ran straight toward us. As he brushed past, I heard a deafening explosion and suddenly I was enveloped in a cloud of feathers. It took a moment before I realized

I had been hit by a bullet from Ruth's rifle. Something wet ran down my hand.

Ruth stared at me in stark terror. With horror she dropped her rifle. "It went off!"

"My God! I'm hit." Then I wondered, "Where did she shoot me?"

I took a deep breath. I could still breathe. My pounding heart was still working. I carefully removed my feather/down vest. Ruth took one look at the blood streaming down my arm and burst into wild sobbing. Frightened, and half-sick with dread, I looked myself over. The bullet had gone through the vest at my side, and it had then made a deep graze in the flesh of the inside of my left forearm. The sight of blood oozing from my arm made me sick and dizzy. "Ruth, give me water, quick," I cried. Then I fainted.

When I recovered consciousness, Ruth had a cold cloth on my head and was bandaging my arm. I said, weakly, "Ruth, your trophy will never make the Boone and Crockett record book. But you hit something, and I missed that bear."

"Will he come back?" she asked, handing me a steaming cup of coffee.

"If he does, we'd better climb a tree."

"Dolores, maybe you hit him."

"Didn't you see him run off like a rabbit? I just scared him."

After the coffee had stiffened my knees, with a tape measure Ruth and I determined that the distance to the bear from where I had fired was exactly 15 feet. The knowledge didn't help. If I couldn't hit a standing bear at that distance, we were really in danger.

We dreaded having to go to bed, but we almost fell asleep over the dying campfire. Then we regretted not having packed in more wood for the cook stove. Neither of us was brave enough to go into the dark forest for more firewood. Shivering with cold, we crawled into our sleeping bag. We had just started to get warm and drowsy, when, somewhere close, wolves howled.

Ruth leaped up. "I'm going to go mad if I have to listen to those wolves all night. There's a horse bell hanging on the saddle rack. Let's tie it up in Jack's spruce tree."

We hung the bell from a branch, and tied a long rope to the bell. A wolf started to howl, and Ruth jerked on the rope, ringing the bell. I also pounded on the dishpan. The racket we made caused the wolf to break off in the middle of a long, low howl. We heard no more wolves for the rest of the night. That night the northern lights were active and bright. We shivered inside, knowing those beautiful lights presaged colder weather. We both needed warmer clothing.

The sun rose bright and warm and wrapped the day in golden glory. With rifles in hand, we tried to find bear tracks of the animal that we had frightened off. We found two leg bones that the bear had gnawed clean of meat. That solved the mystery of the disappearance of the caribou quarter, and of the meatless meat tree. Lucky hadn't been playing pranks with the meat after all.

As we circled back to camp, Ruth yelled. I half-expected to hear her shoot at the bear. Instead, she came running to me waving the red blanket she and Lucky had fought over. "I found where Lucky cached it!" she called, triumphantly.

At camp we struggled to wash by hand the full-sized heavy, wool blanket. When it dried, we decided, we'd make ourselves some shirts. Ruth thought I might have nicked the bold black bear. We feared that the hunters might encounter a wounded bear, so next day we again tried to trail the animal. We scoured all the trails a short distance around camp, but we found nothing. When we returned to camp, Lucky was leaning against the corral, waiting for us.

"Mrs. Brown, how horses?"

"Horses?"

"Yes, Mrs. Brown. Not elephant, not cow, not goat. HORSES. You wrangler now."

Our minds had been so full of bears that neither Ruth nor I had thought of the horses. We glanced at the pole corral and saw dangling ropes. We looked at each other and knew; our five horses had fled when the bear came into camp.

"Lucky, we . . . ."

"Tell Lucky truth," he demanded.

"Well . . . ."

"Did you get the hunters a bear?" Ruth asked, trying to change the subject.

"No bear."

"Where horses?" he asked again. "Heavy frost this morning. Came back by meadow. No horse tracks," he said, accusingly.

"Lucky, where do you suppose the horses went?"

"In Keno now."

"Keno! No. They couldn't!"

"No? Horses go fast. Eat, travel. Eat, travel. All day. All night. In Keno now," he insisted.

In my imagination I saw Louis eating dinner at old Massa's and through the window seeing Baldy, Tootsie, Kate, Jojo and Bobo trotting by.

Lucky shrugged and threw up his hands. "Lucky guide. Lucky wrangler. Lucky do everything." Then he leaped into his saddle and rode off to search for the lost horses. Ruth and I decided that since the hunters did not get a bear, we wouldn't tell them we had shot at one in camp.

Harry and the two hunters came gloomily to supper. Harry reported, "No sheep, no caribou, no bear. Noth'n."

Later Ruth said, in exasperation, "What's the matter with Harry's forty power eyes. This valley is lousy with bears."

We were eating dessert when we heard the five missing horses pound into the clearing, with Lucky whistling and yelling at them from behind. Ruth and I dashed outside and counted. Lucky had found all five. Hurrying to supper, Lucky stumbled across our bell rope, and the bell clanged loudly. He stopped, puzzled, then roared with laughter.

"So, you not scared!"

"We were not!" Ruth flared.

Lucky giggled. "Hear little mice run'n." He yanked on the bell rope until the bell clanged loudly. "Hear little rabbit hopp'n," and the bell rang again.

Ruth demanded, "Why should we be scared when we have two rifles?"

"Lucky not dumb," he said, with a scornful glance.

That night my wounded arm was so painful that I feared blood poisoning had set in. Ruth and I looked in alarm at the red swelling. If the arm became any larger, I would be unable to get my arm into a sleeve. I certainly didn't want the men to know that I had been shot.

Next morning Lucky was chopping wood when he squinted into the sky. "Lots ravens. Why they fly in camp? Noth'n dead here."

Ruth shrugged. "They're waiting for you and Harry to find a bear."

I was stirring soup for lunch when I saw Lucky striding swiftly toward the cook tent. "Lucky's coming, and he looks mad," I warned Ruth.

The tent flaps flipped open and a pair of blazing black eyes flashed at us as Lucky yelled, "Want to know why raven fly around camp? BECAUSE YOU KILL BEAR!"

"But Lucky, I missed him."

"You shoot'm through heart."

"I did? But he ran."

"Hunter be mad as hell now," Lucky shouted.

"But it's only a black bear."

"Black bear, blue bear, green bear, pink bear. Any color bear make hunter happy when he have no bear."

"Don't tell the hunters," I pleaded.

"Tell'm?" Lucky flung up his arms. "They can smell'm! He dead in front of Harry'n my tent. In bushes."

"What was I supposed to do," I yelled. "Let that bear eat me?"

Ruth begged. "Please don't shout. The hunters will hear you."

To my astonishment, Lucky grabbed a dishtowel and sobbed into it, "Harry'n me hunt like hell find bear for hunter. While we gone you shoot'm bear. Not fair."

Ruth snatched back her dishtowel and Lucky covered his face with his hands and his shoulders shook. He gave another racking sob. "You hurt Lucky's feel'n's."

I began to feel badly that I had lost my temper. "Well, I'm sorry." Glancing up, I caught Lucky peeking between his fingers and giving Ruth a broad wink.

"Lucky John, you ham actor. Get out!" I shrieked.

Lucky howled with laughter. "Next time, Mrs. Brown, shoot'm in belly, not heart. T'at way bear not die in front of tent."

I was horrified at that. Louis had taught me that it was important to kill an animal cleanly and quickly.

"Get out so I can cook," I said.

Lucky grinned. "OK Mrs. Brown. But don't shoot any more bears."

"Don't be silly. I have no intention of shooting any more bears."

Little did I know.

More Bear Trouble

With dawn came more ravens. They squawked, quarrelled, and soared in graceful circles over camp. The hunters, at the wash basin in front of their tent, craned their necks following the flight of the black birds. Lucky was near, and Miller called, "Why so many ravens over your tent?"

Lucky shrugged. "Harry throw shoe at little rabbit. He drop dead. Heart attack."

Miller gave Lucky a penetrating look, then resumed brushing his teeth. Shortly, Miller and Dr. Jardine went to the lake to fish briefly before breakfast. Lucky called me outside. He pointed to a big fat raven sitting on a dead snag. "He smell our trouble. Know what I mean?"

I nodded. Lucky indolently leaned against a tree. "Better hurry. Skin 'm bear before he rot."

"Skin the bear? ME?"

"You shoot 'm. You make Harry go back and skin Mr. Ion's crippled bear."

I went into the cook tent. Lucky followed. "You cut'm down middle and . . . ." I hurried outside, looking in a pack box for a can of butter. Lucky, right behind me, said, "Don't forget skin out claws and . . . ." I dashed back into the cook tent. Ruth flipped a hotcake and Lucky grabbed it. He stuffed it into his mouth, and resumed talking, "After you skin 'm, take horse, drag bear carcass out of camp. Harry 'n me don't want him stink'n our tent."

Harry sauntered in for coffee and the two Indians discussed our problem. They decided to take the hunters on another side trip that day while Ruth and I disposed of the bear. When they were packed and mounted I asked, "Harry, how long are you going to be gone!"

He grinned. "One moon."

"You be back in three days," I insisted. "We have to start home soon."

Ruth irritably asked Lucky, "Why are you taking Dina? We'll miss her."

"She all time stay in camp. Maybe you shoot 'm."

They trotted down the trail, and we watched the pack train recede into the distance. When they were safely out of sight, Ruth came out of the cook tent with two large butcher knives. "We have a skinning job. Remember?"

I groaned. "Those knives look awfully clumsy to use for skinning."

Ruth shrugged. "They're all we have. When I wanted to borrow their skinning knives, both Harry and Lucky acted as if I had asked to borrow a million dollars."

I shook my head. "I know. You should have heard Louis scream once when I opened a tin can with his fancy old skinning knife."

We marched up the trail and stopped in front of the Indians' tent. About 16 feet in front of it was a large patch of willows. We struggled through the thick tangle and caught a glimpse of black fur. Smashing down the brush around it, I felt a pang of regret. "Ruth, he looks like a big, fuzzy teddy bear."

Ruth looked at me, puzzled. "For a guide, you're an awful softy."

Ruth raised her knife, "Lucky says to start down the middle."

"Yes. But Ruth, the trick is to see how few holes you cut in the hide."

"Oh, don't be so particular," she said, plunging her knife into the bear's belly. An odoriferous blast of gas escaped with a loud whistle, and we both dashed back to the trail, gagging. With tears in her eyes, Ruth said, "Golly, Dolores, I don't know. We can't skin him the way he smells."

"Maybe a cup of tea will settle our stomachs," I suggested. On the way to the cook tent we passed the trapper's blanket we had washed where it hung, now dry. "Let's cut out a couple of shirts instead," Ruth suggested.

For the rest of the day we labored over two crude shirts for ourselves. Evening arrived, the sun dropped from sight, and we released the horses for their night of grazing.

Next morning, I poked my head out and quickly drew back into the tent. Frost covered the ground. Fog slowly rose from the lake. We could scarcely see the mountains, and what we could see was white. Before we could fill the coffeepot, we had to chop a hole in the ice of the water bucket. Moments later, when I returned for more water, a thin skim of ice had already covered it.

Ruth shivered as she huddled near the stove. "I don't know about you, but after freezing most of the night, I think a nice thick bear rug under us would be wonderful."

"You mean skin that bear?" I asked, shuddering.

"Well, he'd be pretty lumpy to sleep on as he is," Ruth giggled.

"You've been stingy with that fancy cologne of yours. How about pouring some on kerchiefs and tying them around our faces!" I suggested.

"Let's try it," Ruth agreed, jumping to her feet.

We were hacking away at the bear, with a cloud of cologne hovering around our heads, when an object sailed past Ruth's head and landed in my lap. I picked up a large grizzly bear claw, and whirled around to see where it had come from. Lucky was perched on a log. He doubled over with laughter. Gasping for breath he snickered, "You two bad holdup mens. Scare hell out'a Lucky." He rocked on the log with glee.

I jerked the kerchief from my face. "What are you doing back here without the hunters?"

"Kill big grizzly last night!"

"Who?"

"My hunter," Lucky's eyes flashed proudly.

Ruth sighed. "Thank heavens, one of them got a bear."

Lucky walked to his nearby horse and untied a gunnysack from the saddle. "Miller sure happy man."

Ruth asked, "You mean you came back just to bring another bloody bear hide?"

"Sure. You gotta take fat off hide, salt'm, hang up."

"If I ever get this bear skinned, that's enough for me. I'm not going to take your orders," Ruth said, stamping her foot.

Without a word, Lucky unsheathed his skinning knife and while he swiftly skinned out our black bear, Ruth watched to see how it was done. I went to the cook tent to prepare lunch. While we ate, Lucky told us about Miller's grizzly. "First shot, he shoot'm in paw. That give bear time hide in bushes. Hard tell how far bear gone. Me 'n' Harry track'm til we hear growl. Miller right behind. He say, 'You fellows better shoot.'

"Bear charge. Miller shoot his second shot. He yell 'shoot!' Me 'n' Harry wait for Miller shoot again. Bang, he shoot. Bear keep com'n. T'en we all shoot. Bear drop. Dead. T'at sure one big grizzly."

"Dr. Jardine good sport, but he a little sick he have no bear," Lucky confided. Then, turning to Ruth, he teased, "T'is morning breakfast, Lucky cook lots good stuff for hunter, me. Toast, hotcakes, biscuits, and . . . ."

"Lucky, you're lying," Ruth said as she threw a cinnamon roll at him.

Hooting with laughter, he dodged. Then he said, "Got to catch Harry and outfit before they get big river." Quickly, he showed us how to flesh the two bear hides. He left his skinning knife for us to use, admonishing, "Leave little teeth marks on knife 'n Lucky sure use big willow stick." He meant that if we nicked the cutting edge of his knife, he was going to be angry enough to thrash us both.

After Lucky left, Ruth and I tried to hitch a horse to the skinned black bear carcass to pull it away from camp. Not one of the horses would get near the bear. We finally left it where it was and covered it with brush and moss. We worked late by the light of the campfire. After we had carefully cut all the fat and flesh from the hides, we salted them heavily and rolled them up.

We were dead tired when we went to bed and next morning we slept later than usual. We had to retrieve the grazing horses, but before leaving, we hung Mr. Miller's grizzly skin on a rope near his tent where he could admire it. We preferred that the hunters not see the black bear hide, so we found an old game trail and hung it across a nearby small clearing.

We took our time going after the horses, for highbush cranberries grew thickly along the way, and we sampled them as we walked. We crossed a small stream that was dark with swimming grayling. At the grazing meadow usually used by the horses, a bull moose snorted and trotted across the flat, his big antlers glistening in the sunshine. Two cow caribou stood and looked curiously at us before gracefully trotting off.

There was no sign of the horses. We walked to the end of the meadow and found their tracks. They had crossed a creek, heading south. We decided to climb a ridge where we could have a good view of the creek valley. Lowbush cranberries nestled like blood-red rubies on the pale green and velvety moss of the hillside. We climbed higher. A fire had once swept through the spruces here, and among the charred stumps and fallen trees we found thick clusters of red currants. From atop the ridge we caught a glimpse of a moving animal on a game trail far below. We decided it was one of the missing horses, so we climbed down and followed the trail where it wound along a creek.

Still, we couldn't find the horses. We climbed again to gain a better view. The hillside was covered with blueberries, tear-shaped and delicately frosted with a silvery sheen. We sat amidst a patch, gorging ourselves. Then I heard the crack of a breaking stick. I looked up and my blood froze. "Ruth," I whispered, "Don't move. Look up, slowly."

Ruth gasped. Not 50 yards away, and peering down on us, was a large grizzly bear. Ruth whirled. "My rifle, where's my rifle?" I backed slowly to the birch tree where I had leaned my .270. I eased a shell into the chamber and waited. Behind me, I heard Ruth still seeking her rifle. I stood ready, watching every move of the bear. I didn't want to kill him. This was his berry patch. We were intruders. I marked a downed tree as the nearest distance I would allow the bear without shooting. The bear stood on his hind legs. I lowered my rifle, thinking that he was simply curious. However, when he dropped to all fours again, that big hump-shouldered grizzly immediately charged down the slope, straight for us.

I slammed my rifle to my shoulder and followed the leaping bear with it. He gained speed on the steep slope. When he leaped the downed tree I had marked, I fired at him, yanked the bolt back, shoved another cartridge into place, and again fired.

The grizzly fell over, kicking violently then rolled over. Moments later he leaped to his feet and disappeared into the brush and timber.

Ruth, big-eyed, standing beside me with her unfired rifle, said, "My God. He charged us!" And then, "Did you miss?"

"No. I heard at least one bullet connect."

"It looks as if we have a tracking job," I said, shakily.

The last thing in the world I wanted to do was to track a wounded grizzly in thick brush. I had no idea how badly he was wounded. We looked for blood, and I found a red splash on some feathery moss. Drops of blood led us the edge of a ravine. We looked down into a tangle of willow, alder, and dwarf spruce.

"Since I have a guide's license, you know what I'm obligated to do, don't you?" I asked Ruth.

"If you go into that thicket you'll not only be a dumb guide, but a dead one. Let's circle the ravine and look down into it," she suggested.

We clawed our way over logs and boulders. Every few feet we stopped to throw rocks into the brush below, trying to flush the bear. We heard a sudden clicking on a shale slope and swiveled about, rifles ready. It was only three caribou that we had startled. They fled into thick timber.

We had to cross a deep, swift stream. Wet to our waists, we fought through fallen timber. My heart leaped at every sound. When Ruth stepped on a stick and it broke I whirled about, rifle ready, thinking the bear was charging. I glared at Ruth.

We reached the high side of the ravine and peered down. "That's an odd-colored rock," Ruth commented.

"It's not a rock. It's the bear," I gasped.

"Do you think he's playing possum?"

"The Indians say that grizzlies will, sometimes."

With rocks large and small we pelted the prone and still bear, and the area around him. He didn't move.

"Ruth, you stay here with your rifle ready. I'm going down."

"No way. We go together."

When we were within ten feet of the bear, I had Ruth stop and keep her rifle aimed at the animal while I sneaked close and poked him with my rifle. There was no response, no movement. The grizzly was dead.

Ruth lifted one of the giant paws. "This bear is huge! It'll take us all day to skin him."

"I'm glad you watched Lucky and learned how," I said.

"Ruth sighed. I brought Lucky's skinning knife to clean fish. I never dreamed I'd need it for a bear."

I had a sharp pocketknife, and between us we started to work. It proved to be a tremendous task to remove that vast, thick bear skin. We had to use pry poles to turn the bear over. We tugged, pulled, pushed, and heaved. Soon we were wet with perspiration.

Ruth poked her knife into a hole near the bear's shoulder. "Dolores, the bullet went in . . . ."

"Stop! I can't stand to hear bear hunters tell where the bullet went in, and how much blood spurted out!"

"Well, anyway," Ruth finished lamely, "it's good that you didn't miss."

The hide was too heavy to carry. We needed a horse. We rolled it and tied it with our bootlaces. Ruth hung her red scarf to mark where we left it, and we went down to the floor of the valley, looking for the strayed horses. Long shadows told us that evening was near. We couldn't find the horses, so we decided to go back to camp and return in the morning. Both of us were dead tired. We weren't sure in which direction camp lay, and we stood debating which way to go when we heard a horse bell.

After straining our ears for a time, Ruth ran up on a knoll. "I'm sure it's Copper's little bell. Hear it?" she called.

Far across the flat we saw a string of approaching horses. The hunters!

I warned Ruth, "I hold a general hunting license and I can legally shoot a black bear and a grizzly, but it is unethical for a guide to kill game when with a hunting party."

Ruth nodded. "I understand. If Dr. Jardine still doesn't have a grizzly, it would be terribly embarrassing. Mum's the word. Now, I wonder how we're going to get that hide back to camp without anyone seeing it."

The horses drew near, and we saw with them the lost horses that Ruth and I had sought. We ran down the hill and waited. Harry led two of the strays, and Dr. Jardine the other. Two other horses had empty saddles.

"Where are Lucky and Mr. Miller?" I asked Harry, when they got close.

Harry reined in, "They walk'n over mountain. Hunt sheep."

On Dina's back was a set of huge caribou antlers. "Who got those?" I asked.

Dr. Jardine answered, proudly, "I did. Aren't they beautiful?"

Ruth and I swung up on the two saddled horses and I told Harry, "We have to go back after our pack. We'll follow you soon."

As the packtrain went on, I asked Ruth, "Two of the horses are limping. Did you notice?"

"I sure did. Harry looks kind of funny, and he's lost his hat," she said.

"Something is wrong," I guessed.

We rode to the grizzly hide. We tied Lady up at the mouth of the ravine, and worked old Baldy through the thickets to the rolled-up hide. A gunnysack was tied to Baldy's saddle, and we shoved the bear hide into it. Most of the latigo strings were missing, and we used our belts to strap the hide to the saddle. Baldy was such an old hand at hunting, that he didn't blink an eye. Not wanting to sit on the bloody hide, I rode double behind Ruth.

We trotted the horses most of the way back to camp. Near camp we heard a wild commotion—hoarse shouts, loud banging. We rounded a turn in the trail in time to see duffel bags and pack boxes flying.

"Hang on!" I yelled to Ruth, as the horse we rode passed the black bear hide we had hung in the trail. It shied, and dashed into camp, with Baldy close behind.

We came to an abrupt stop. Harry was wandering about, wobbly and limping. Dr. Jardine, looking dazed, asked, "What scared the horses?"

I didn't dare tell him it was the black bear hide hanging near the trail.

"Did Harry get bucked off? Is he hurt?"

Dr. Jardine hesitantly replied, "Well, yes, and no. The fact is, Harry is sick."

"Sick?!"

Jardine chuckled. "Well, we sort of had a little rodeo last night, and Harry got bucked off a couple of times, and . . . ."

A piercing whistle came, and I looked up. It was Lucky. He and Mr. Miller were partway down the mountain, headed for camp. Lucky cupped his hands and yelled, "COFFEE!"

"OK," Ruth answered as she headed for the cook tent.

Lucky came in laughing. I bounced him. "Harry's sick, hurt, or something. What happened? What did you do?"

His laughter died, and the small muscles around his mouth twitched. I was so angry I trembled. "Some of the horses are limping. They're crippled. You are responsible for those horses. What happened?"

"Last night hunters gave Harry little drink. Harry feel pretty good. Harry make horses buck. Show hunters him good rider. Not Harry fault. He have to be good sport, make hunters happy," he said. Then, with great dignity, Lucky walked out.

Ruth rushed after him with the coffeepot. "Take this and pour it down Harry. ALL OF IT."

I was pretty sure Lucky hadn't told all. It is common for hunters to have liquor on hunts. Louis refused to provide booze for his hunts, saying he didn't object if his clients wanted to bring along their own bottle or two for light social drinking.

Dr. Jardine and Mr. Miller probably felt embarrassed about leaving Harry out when they had an evening drink. They had decided to include him, not realizing that their generosity might jeopardize their hunt. So far, Harry had been a wonderful guide. But if the hunters continued to share their liquid assets, this hunting party was going to be bogged down for sure.

The Hard Trail Home

When the bright sun started to melt morning frost next morning, the two hunters were up early, eager to hunt. Unfortunately, there was a problem, Dr. Jardine's guide was nowhere to be seen. Surprised and disappointed, Dr. Jardine anxiously asked, "Do you suppose Harry didn't hear the call to breakfast?"

I smiled. "He heard."

"Maybe you better go and get him up," he suggested.

"Under the circumstances, I believe the responsibility is yours," I said, looking the good doctor hard in the eye. Both hunters went to the Indians' tent and soon returned, announcing that Harry was very ill.

"And whose fault is that?" I asked, sweetly.

To his credit, Dr. Jardine admitted his responsibility. Both apologized for giving Harry liquor. "No more whiskey for Harry from us," they promised.

Ruth served a platter of fragrant ham and eggs. Miller asked, "Mrs. Brown, what lake does the bush pilot pick us up from?"

Lucky paused with a forkful of ham halfway to his mouth. Ruth lowered her eyes. Now was the time to break the news, I decided, and I drew a big breath and took the plunge. "We're all riding out. All the small lakes are starting to freeze early."

"How about hunting?"

"Good all the way back to Keno."

"That's fine. We'll get to see more of the country."

Lucky's fork continued its journey, and I relaxed.

Miller suggested, "Why don't we start back right away and take more time hunting?"

"Good idea," I agreed with relief. "We'll start packing today, and we'll leave as soon as Harry can travel."

"How many days to Keno?" Dr. Jardine asked.

"Oh, about three," I answered.

The hunters left the tent. "We'll fish today and give Harry time to recover."

Shortly Lucky cornered me. "You think Lucky take you Keno on magic carpet?"

"What do you mean, Lucky?"

"No way, three day. You tell hunter three day back."

"Old Jack said it was."

"That man's shortcut. Think horses goats? Fly over peaks?"

"You and Harry made it in three days."

"Me 'n' Harry travel day 'n' night. Days longer then."

It was true, the days of autumn were now noticeably shorter than when we had arrived in the valley. "Then you tell the hunters we'll be home for Christmas," I snapped, as I watched a pale and shaky Harry come down the trail. He certainly looked ill, and I wondered if he had a resurgence of his old stomach ailment. Ruth silently fixed him broth and poached an egg, but he didn't feel any better. Desperately anxious to get started on the homeward trail, I gave him another dose of Dr. Bell's horse medicine.

Ruth started to fill the pack boxes, and Lucky teased her by tossing on top of the flour, rice, and other foodstuffs, his shoeing hammer, axes and horseshoes. She screamed, "Lucky, get your hardware junk out of my kitchen boxes." Lucky snickered, "Gotta pack horse stuff."

Seeing that a battle was brewing, I told Lucky to mend some broken halters and horse hobbles. That night after everyone had turned in, Ruth and I cared for the hide of the grizzly that had charged us. We felt certain that if it grew any colder we would need a bearskin on top as well as underneath us at night.

Camp was a turmoil before dawn. Harry helped Lucky saddle the horses. While the hunters fished the lake for the last time, Ruth and I knocked down the tents, and emptied the stove of ashes. We stacked everything beside the saddle rack. Lucky looked at the huge pile of camp gear, luggage, and trophies. He scratched his head.

"You think Lucky magician?" he querulously asked me.

"If you can pack Big Dan, maybe you can do it. But even then I doubt it," I said.

Lucky was piqued. "You think Lucky not able pack Dan?"

"Louis is the only one who has ever been able to pack him."

Lucky was determined to show me he could load everything on the horses. As Harry led each horse to the pile and Lucky hooked and tied items on, the pile began to shrink. Finally, only one horse was left. Big Dan was so large that he could easily carry everything left on the ground. He dwarfed Lucky and Harry. Harry tied his halter rope to a tree, and Lucky swung a pack box up and hooked it on the packsaddle. Harry, on the other side of the horse, grabbed another box, balanced it on his knee to get a firmer grip, and swung it up. Unfortunately, something rattled in the box. Dan used that as an excuse to lunge wildly. Harry dropped the box and leaped away from the plunging horse, and I followed. We had no desire to be brained by one of those big hoofs.

Lucky sidestepped the plunging animal and talked to the nervous horse. "Dan, you my friend. Now you behave. I don't trust you, Dan. You too damn big, too damn strong. You stubborn sonofabitch, and I make you behave. Now, Dan, you hold still, let Lucky load you."

As he talked, half cussing the horse, trying to gentle him, he stepped close and eased the pack box off and swung it aside. Dan bunched his powerful muscles and leaped forward. Then he flung himself back, breaking the halter rope. Kicking and bucking, he raced past the other patiently waiting and loaded packhorses.

Lucky followed and lassoed him, and led him back. He then used a choke rope to try to control the fighting horse. Dan used all of his brute force to bite and kick at Lucky, who adroitly dodged, and spoke gently to the raging animal.

Ruth thought that Lucky was showing off. She commented, "If we're going to make the next camp before dark, we can't stand here all day watching a rodeo. This pile of baggage isn't going to get any smaller by looking at it."

Dan won. We decided it would take too long to subdue and pack him. Even if Lucky did get him loaded, he would probably buck his load off or wreck it in some other way. We stood helplessly looking at the supplies that still lay piled on the ground.

"Cache it in tree," Lucky advised.

"Not my cook stove," yelped Ruth.

Harry spoke. "Old time Indian, he not have stove. Cook over fire."

We cached the stove, one tent, and most of the horseshoeing equipment. Noon arrived before we started on the homeward trail. Miller, having been over the trail through the pass, led the way. Harry shouldered a pack and started on foot. Lucky rode through the brush and gathered up scattered horses. I gritted my teeth as the white giant, Big Dan, galloped by with not one thing on his broad, strong back, while all the smaller horses sagged under their loads.

Ruth and I stopped to take a last look at *Neechemoos*. The valley stretched peacefully to distant, remote peaks. Wild swans floated on the lake's tranquil surface. Several white specks—Dall sheep—grazed on a grassy knoll. Several caribou trotted along the beach on the far shore. We had come to love this beautiful place, and we both knew it would remain in our hearts and minds forever. Old Jack had been right; this valley was a very special place.

Copper pranced past, carrying Lucky's saddle. I wished he were old enough to be ridden. Harry and Lucky were taking turns walking and riding one horse—Lady. Ruth's horse Bobo was as slow as a snail, and she was forever being left behind. This tickled Lucky, and he often rode his horse facing backward so could look at Ruth. Once he composed a song for her.

"Who that prospector follow'n us

Don't like snuff, don't drink liquor, or cuss

Never find gold a'rid'n slow Bobo

Not even keep up with ol' Jojo

Claims all staked time they get there.

Poor ol' prospector . . . ."

Lady lunged up a steep bank, and Lucky's legs shot down to save himself from being pitched off. Ruth gaily laughed.

The trail wound close to the edge of a deep canyon. Sheep trails intersected the main trail. Occasionally a horse had to plunge and heave up steep pitches to keep on the trail. The packtrain started to descend the mountain, after crossing a high divide, and Lucky thoughtfully let Harry ride while he walked, carrying his guitar. The rugged, snowy peaks made a spectacular backdrop for the picturesque packtrain. Ruth and I were amused as the horses flicked their ears about, listening to their wrangler's serenade. With his huge cowboy hat wobbling on the back of his head and his chaps flapping with every step, Lucky took short-cuts through the brush to get ahead. He popped out from behind a tree, a knoll, or some brush, to loudly strum the guitar to us as we rode by.

As we descended, we left the rocky trail behind, and the horses began to sink into deep moss. Harry called, "Better walk." It was too late. Bunny lunged belly-deep in a muskeg patch. The reins flew out of my hands and I had to cling to the leaping horse's mane. When Bunny reached firm ground again, Mr. Miller, still on his horse, reached down and handed me my reins. I appreciated this, and thanked him for it.

Lucky happened to see this. He managed to catch Ruth's Bobo as he was emerging from the muskeg. He yanked the reins out of Ruth's hand. Ruth reached for the fallen reins, and Lucky jerked them out of her reach. Then, with exaggerated movements, he handed the reins back to Ruth, saying, "Lucky some gentleman!"

Harry's sharp eyes, now properly focused after his night of celebration, spotted five rams sleeping atop a ridge. We made camp, so the hunters could try for the rams the next day. Ruth and I then had our first taste of setting up a six-person camp after eight hours in the saddle. While the Indians finished unpacking and taking care of the horses, Ruth and I struggled to erect the cook tent. We got it pitched all right, although it did lean a bit to one side. The hunters' tent was smaller and easier to put up. Ruth gathered wood while I cooked supper over the campfire. I came out of the smoke with frizzled bangs, which I detested.

The good weather held. Next morning was cool, crisp, and clear. Every blade of grass, ever willow leaf, sparkled with dazzling white frost. I peeked out of the tent to see three saddled horses shivering in the pale yellow rays of the sun. I breathed deeply, then sniffed. I smelled coffee, and the fragrant aroma of bacon. I peeked under the back of our tent to see Harry and Lucky bent over the campfire, cooking breakfast. How good they are, I thought, as I felt of my singed hair. By the time Ruth and I were about and hovering over the campfire, Miller and Lucky were mounted. Miller waved and called, "I bet I get a ram."

After the dishes were washed, there was nothing to do, so we put our sleeping bag in front of the fire and crawled in. Suddenly, my shoulder was being shaken, and Lucky was yelling, "What's matter? You sleep all day? Come see Miller's ram!"

Mr. Miller was very happy. He had collected a fine old ram that carried a beautifully proportioned set of horns. I was consoled by the thought that the old ram probably would not have survived another winter, for his teeth were worn almost to the gums.

Next campsite was to be at Moose Pasture—a long, hard day's ride. Ruth and I started breaking camp early the morning after the successful sheep hunt. As the horses came running into the clearing, Harry and Ruth caught and tied them to trees. Ruth came to tell me that Copper was missing. Nor had Lucky returned from herding the horses back to camp.

I groaned. "That's the way it always is, when you want an early start, a horse is always missing." From a distance came a merry tinkling of a bell. Ruth cocked her ear. "That's Copper's bell. It seems to be going in a circle."

"Sounds jerky," I observed.

Just then Copper pranced into the clearing with Lucky firmly seated on his back. Lucky saw us and waved. Copper, with arched neck, each hoof springing high, mane flying, danced toward us. How graceful, I thought, and what a pair!

Lucky swung off and Copper nosed my shoulder to be petted. My heart was bursting with pride. "Why, Copper, you're a grown up horse now. You've been ridden for the first time."

Lucky lovingly petted him. "Only ride him little bit, sometimes. Don't want to hurt young horse."

I doused the campfire with water as the packtrain left the clearing. I hurriedly climbed on a stump and stepped into my saddle. I leaned over to retie my rifle scabbard, and my body lurched as the saddle started to slide. I hung suspended between the ground and Bunny's belly. Desperately, I clung to Bunny's mane. I tried to jerk my foot loose, but it had slipped through the stirrup. My wool shirt was hooked over the pommel of the saddle. I could feel Bunny's muscles bunching, and her ears drew back. I knew real fear. If she bolted, I'd be dragged.

"Dolores, Dolores," I heard Ruth call. She was riding back to look for me. "Dolor. . .LUCKY, LUCKY, COME QUICK!" she screamed, and I knew she had seen my dilemma.

"Yes, Ruth. Com'n," Lucky responded.

"HURRY!" Ruth screamed.

Bunny reared, and I swung under her. I caught a glimpse of Lucky's boots as he arrived and with firm hands held Bunny's head. He talked softly, "Whoa Bunny, that good girl. Steady."

Bunny lunged, and Lucky held her bridle. Ruth half pulled me out from under the plunging horse, jerked my foot through the stirrup, and untangled my shirt. When Lucky saw I was all right, he said, "Mrs. Brown, you have close call."

Bunny and I both shook with fright. Lucky resaddled her, making sure the cinch was tight. Then he told me, "Try catch up with packtrain. They follow creek. Harry, he go up mountain."

Lucky was afoot, and Ruth was riding slow Bobo. It was up to me to catch the loaded packhorses as they wound their way up a caribou trail. Harry and the two hunters were far in the distance, hunting high on the mountain. I caught up with the packtrain, finally, and tried to hold them until Lucky arrived. Shortly, I heard Copper's little bell and then here came Copper, feet flying as he danced past, with Lucky sitting him with ease.

We turned the horses and started up the mountain. Lucky refused to ride Copper up the mountain. "Too hard on young horse," he explained, as he easily trotted along in the wake of the packtrain. Two eagles soared high above the peaks, and we watched them with envy. How easy it seemed. Then eight caribou bounced across a gully ahead. They nervously circled downwind to get our scent. When they caught our smell, they leaped into a frightened run.

Ruth lagged far behind and I was afraid she would become lost. I returned to her and led Bobo at a faster pace. Windfalls cluttered the trails, and rain started. Lucky seemed to be shouting from all directions, as he kept the scattering horses headed in the right direction.

Ruth and I came upon Tootsie with her pack under her belly. She stood patiently waiting for someone to help. Ruth and I were unpacking her when Lucky called, "Where you?"

"HERE," Ruth answered.

He found us and helped us repack. He was worried. "Mrs. Brown. Keep up with horses."

The day was wearing on. Surely, Harry would stop at the next clearing to give us time to round up the packstring and count them. Suddenly Bunny sank beneath me, and I heard the saddle cinch snap as we hit a pothole.

I managed to drag the saddle away from where she lay, and coax Bunny to her feet and back to a level spot. As I worked with her, Copper trotted up. The saddle was heavy, and impossible for me to swing back onto Bunny. I had to ease it up her side inch-by-inch. Relieved that

I finally had the saddle back atop the horse, I turned to see where Ruth was when I heard a *plunk* behind me. Copper had nosed the saddle off! When I couldn't catch Copper, I tried to chase him away, but he kept coming back to tease Bunny.

Ruth and Lucky heard me speaking harshly to Copper, and came crashing through the underbrush. "Something wrong, Mrs. Brown?"

"Yes. Plenty."

We were in rough country, where the walking was difficult. Lucky said, tiredly, "Pretty nice have Lucky popping out of bushes to help!"

Ruth was exasperated. "We've been six hours on the trail and we haven't seen hide nor hair of Harry. I've called and called for him to stop. Lucky and I have to finish repacking Jim and Prince."

"Rain make rope loose," Lucky explained. Then, always bubbling with energy and fun, he kidded, "Pretty soon at Moose Meadows. Find jam!"

Ruth said, "I could eat a whole case of jam right now. I need a ton of energy to finish this day."

Lucky finished saddling my horse and I swung up. He slapped Bunny. "Mrs. Brown, ride like hell. Catch Harry. Say lots trouble."

I tried to find a good caribou trail, and while searching I came across Dr. Jardine's large suitcase where it had fallen from a packhorse. I hung my red scarf in a tree above it to mark the spot. Farther along, I came upon Buck, lying on his side, bogged down. I left him where he was, hoping that Ruth and Lucky would find him. I came to a hard-packed caribou trail, and brought Bunny to a gallop. As she ducked and jumped fallen logs, the branch of a spruce tree slapped my face with a stinging blow. Suddenly Bunny slid to a stop, and I almost went over her head.

The good trail ended in a ravine that was filled with a recent slide of oozing black mud, uprooted trees, and huge boulders. My heart leaped. Queen, another of our packhorses, was helplessly sinking into this quagmire a full 10 feet from hard ground.

I threw brush on the mud and crawled to her and cut the pack ropes. She struggled, and fell back. It was impossible for me to get her out alone.

Shaking with fury, I jumped on Bunny and sped up the side of the ravine, following Harry's tracks. Lather flew from Bunny's flanks. If I ever caught Harry, I would skin him alive. Just wait until I caught Harry . . . .

Trophies Bagged

"HARRY, HARRY," I screamed.

A flock of half-white ptarmigan flushed with cackles and a roar from the brush, and Bunny shied. Her sides were heaving when we reached the top of the ridge. We tore along the crest. "HARRY."

Finally, I heard an answer.

"STOP. STOP!" I yelled.

I caught up with Trigger. The caribou antlers on top of his pack were tilted and a sharp antler point was gouging his side. Drops of blood rolled down his belly and dripped onto the ground. Ahead, Harry and the hunters waited for me. I jerked Bunny to a sliding stop beside the guide. "Why in blazes didn't you wait for us?"

Mr. Miller laughed. "We thought you were having a good time back there."

I glared at Harry. He sat sagging in his saddle, puffing a cigarette. He returned my stare from sullen, half-closed eyes. I screeched, "Do you think you're running an express train? Look at Trigger, being gored by that caribou antler! Jim and Prince have lost their packs. Queen is stuck in the mud, and so is Buck!"

I was so angry that I lost my voice.

I didn't realize that Harry wasn't surly. He was frightened by my behavior. In his culture, the belief is that anyone who loses his temper—as I was doing—was becoming insane. There is a deep fear of the insane. It is to Harry's credit that he didn't vanish into the bush. Also, I didn't fully understand that Harry had his hands full with two hunters. Their burning desire was to shoot a trophy that would win them a Boone and Crockett Club award. They were unconcerned with the problems of scattered and bogged-down packhorses.

Harry dismounted without a word and went to Trigger and adjusted the caribou antlers. As I stood fuming, watching Harry work with Trigger,

I was surprised to see Dick and Prince trot into view. Their packs were still solidly in place. Behind them, I heard Ruth and Lucky urging them along.

Then came a hoarse shout of warning from Lucky. Ruth screamed. Bobo bolted, terrified, kicking and bucking into the underbrush. Ruth, on his back, flopped about like a rag doll, trying to hang on. She screamed with fright. I dug my heels into Bunny and met Lucky, afoot, as he ran toward Bobo. He was gasping for breath. He pulled me from the saddle and leaped onto Bunny, and headed on a dead run for the bucking Bobo. I screamed after him, "Don't let Ruth drag, don't let her drag." I feared that Bobo would buck her off, and that she might fall off with a foot caught in a stirrup.

I ran and stumbled through the brush to where I had last seen the bucking Bobo, and came upon Lucky kneeling over a huddled Ruth. He looked up and grinned, "My friend here sure give Lucky bad scare."

"Ruth, are you hurt?" I asked, gently.

She raised her head and smiled wanly. "No. I don't think so."

Lucky grinned in relief. "Mrs. Brown, she fall on soft moss. She stay with Bobo about six buck jumps. She sure good cowboy rider. Take her to next rodeo."

With flaming cheeks Ruth howled with hysterical laughter. I managed a frozen smile. "What happened?" Lucky explained. "Lucky find bag of salt on trail, fall off packhorse. Give Ruth. She tie on saddle, but she not tie tight. Salt fall off, scare Bobo."

He turned to Ruth, "My friend all right?"

Ruth jumped up, "Of course."

Lucky mounted Bunny and rode after the frightened Bobo. He soon returned, leading the nervous horse, minus saddle and blanket. He then left with Harry to pull Queen and Buck out of the mud. Ruth and I searched for Bobo's lost saddle and blanket.

Somehow we all reached the Moose Pasture, our planned overnight campsite. It was amidst a series of large open meadows, lush with yellow cured grass. Surrounding the meadows was a stand of large spruce trees. Beyond were the snowy peaks of the Ogilvie Mountains. Far below, along a deep, winding stream, were flats thickly matted with wolf willows—the bedding and feeding grounds of moose.

The hunters explored the area while Ruth and I unpacked the horses as they wandered into camp one by one. We pitched tents, built a fire, and started supper. Ruth shoved a pan of bannock into the reflector oven, sighing, "Oh, for some jam or jelly to spread on this."

"This is where that old prospector supposedly cached two cases of jam," I reminded her.

"Where?" Ruth asked.

"Let's start looking," I suggested.

We found a scattered pile of cans. Ruth exploded,"I just hate litter-bugs. Why do campers leave a mess like this? I'd like to kick 'em in the seat of their pants."

"And I'd love to see you do it," I smiled, picking up one of the cans.

"You would?" Ruth asked, in surprise.

I laughed. "I sure would. You'd be kicking a 500-pound grizzly bear!"

Ruth's eyes widened. "Grizzly?"

"Look," I said, handing her a can, "All these holes were made by big teeth. The bears beat us to the jam."

Harry and Lucky arrived with Buck and Queen. Ruth asked Lucky, "Did you ever see so many things happen in one day?"

Lucky laughed. "Big show. Just like rodeo. Lucky pickup man today."

It turned bitterly cold. Under bright moonlight we hurriedly finished washing dishes. Ruth was filling a hot water bottle from a pan of heated water when Lucky snatched the bottle from her hand. He dashed to an ice-rimmed pond and dipped the bottle in. With a shriek, Ruth went after him. Whooping with shouts of laughter, Lucky dodged and raced across the moon-drenched meadow. Frost sparkled at his feet. The two lively youngsters darted in and out of the shadows around the campfire. I was to long remember this scene of joyous youth and freedom.

Before going to bed, I went to Dina where she stood at the edge of the firelight. I pressed my cheek against her soft, silky neck. She was so warm, sweet, and gentle. I wondered what Louis was doing at that moment. After the happenings of the day, I wondered if I would get back to him alive.

Ruth and I awoke near midnight, shivering. "I hope we stay here long enough to dry our bear skins," she said, as we lay close together, seeking warmth from each other. Next time we awoke, Harry was pounding freshly fallen snow from our tent. Covering my head, I groaned and rolled over. Ruth muttered, "Let's hibernate."

The strong fragrant odor of wood smoke drifted through the tent flaps, and I heard the cheery crackling of the fire. Two steaming cups of coffee were pushed under the tent wall. "Hurry, wake up, get breakfast. Harry'n me go'n take hunters on side trip for caribou and bear."

Moaning over our fate, Ruth and I sipped the hot black liquid. Sleepiness began to leave. However, one look through the tent flaps at all the white snow on pans, boxes and kettles made us shudder at the thought of cooking breakfast.

With chattering teeth we fumbled with cold pans. The bacon was so cold and stiff that Harry had to chop it with an axe. Lucky held a loaf of bread over the fire to thaw; it was as hard as a rock.

"Go'n get Miller big caribou rack today," Lucky proclaimed.

"Stop bragging," Ruth warned.

Lucky's eyes flashed. "You t'ink Lucky lie?"

"At least you have a good imagination," Ruth said.

"Get Miller one giant caribou," Lucky insisted.

"And Harry will get a big grizzly for Dr. Jardine," I said. "Won't you, Harry?"

Harry, a forgiving soul, grinned and nodded. He was still a bit wary of me after my blowup.

Before leaving, Lucky warned, "Watch out for Tootsie. She smart. You still wrangler, you know, Mrs. Brown."

After the hunters had left, Ruth and I hung up our bear skins near the fire, to finish drying. The raw, cold air penetrated our thin summer weight clothing. The previous day's ride through thick brush had wreaked havoc with our already-worn jeans and shirts.

"We're going to look like hags," Ruth said, pulling her hair back in mock horror.

"Or a toothless hag," I said, wiggling a front tooth with my tongue.

"What ever happened?" Ruth asked, peering into my mouth.

"When I was a youngster, I was in an apricot tree, gorging myself. My nursemaid came to get me. I refused to climb down. She came right up after me. In my excitement I fell, and when I landed, the apricot pit in my mouth punched my front tooth out."

"And now the bridge is loose?" Ruth asked.

"It happened yesterday," I said. "And I'd just die if I lost it."

With sweaters we each made a crude pair of long underwear. We swiped another of Lucky's horse blankets, and without bothering to wash it this time, we quilted it between a couple of cotton blouses. Enough was left to make two pair of long wool socks. Our new clothing, though crude, and smelling of horse, was warm. This lifted our spirits.

We searched for the grazing horses, and moved them nearer to camp. Soon we saw a bull moose grazing among them. Across the valley we watched three large bull caribou on the mountain.

Ruth was gathering firewood when she whooped and came running, holding a can up. "I found a good can of jam under a big bushy spruce," she said, triumphantly.

"Why Ruth, it's strawberry. My favorite."

Ruth made a bannock, and under bright moonlight we sat around the campfire and spread gobs of jam on large wedges of hot bannock. We didn't stop eating until the whole one pound can was empty. With satisfied appetites, and cuddled between two dry bearskins, we slept the sleep of innocence.

Ruth woke me in the morning. "Dolores, I don't hear horse bells. I'll bet they've headed back for that goose grass."

"I better ride Tootsie after them before they get too far," I said, grabbing my clothes.

Hanging limply from a branch was an empty halter. "Tootsie is gone!" I gasped.

Ruth groaned. "That means walking. While you fix our lunch, I'll climb that knoll and see if I can spot them."

I scribbled a note and hung it on the tip of a branch to let the hunters know where we had gone. I put some bannock and beans in a sack, and was readying to leave when I turned and almost screamed when I saw someone standing there.

"Lucky! You scared me!"

"Yes, Mrs. Brown. Lucky came back. Mrs. Brown, look. See what on Baldy."

I stared in astonishment and Lucky grinned. "Teach Ruth Lucky not lie. Lucky dependable. Lucky good hunter, like Louis."

Atop Baldy's pack was the largest set of caribou antlers I had ever seen. They were symmetrical and beautiful, with many points. The shovel was long, and it fanned out into a flare of symmetrical points. That set of antlers was to win for Mr. Miller the 56th place in the 1958 Boone and Crockett book of Records of North American Big Game.

Lucky spied my note flapping in the breeze and jerked it off. "So, Mrs. Brown, you let Tootsie outsmart you?"

"How did she slip her halter?" I wondered.

"So. She play trick on you. Tell you she smart."

"Where's Harry?"

"He come'n. Dr. Jardine one happy man."

"Oh. What did they get?" I asked.

Lucky refused to tell me. "Harry, Dr. Jardine, tell you," he said.

He finished unpacking Baldy. "Give Lucky little bite to eat. Maybe go after horses."

Ruth returned and said she had seen the horses working their way downhill near the mud slide. Lucky took off after them. He returned with all the horses, then he insisted that Ruth take a hundred feet of movie film of him with the huge caribou antlers.

"T'at always remind you, Ruth. Lucky not brag. Lucky tell truth when he say get big caribou," he told her.

Harry and Dr. Jardine arrived in the late afternoon. Dr. Jardine was so excited he could hardly talk. He called us, "Come see my silvertip. He's a beauty."

He spoke the truth. The grizzly he had killed was huge, and it squared almost nine feet (average of greatest length and greatest width of the hide). The claws, which looked like gray ivory, were as long as my hand. The fur was thick and so long it gently waved with every breeze, and it shimmered with a silvery sheen.

I beamed at Harry. "Louis said you were a wonderful guide. I'm proud you found this grizzly for Dr. Jardine. It must be the biggest grizzly in the Yukon."

With two additional trophies, some of our load had to be left in a cache. Harry warned, "Trail bad. Maybe better cache everyt'ing."

Next morning before leaving we cached the table, half of the pack boxes, our tent and the cook tent, all shoeing equipment, and all the iron pots and pans.

We were busily breaking camp when Miller and Dr. Jardine told me they had all the trophies they wanted, and that they would as soon head right for Mayo. They wanted to hunt for moose, but, they said, they could hunt moose at our ranch.

Lucky and Harry whooped, joked, and laughed as they packed the horses. They would be seeing their girlfriends sooner than expected.

Frozen moss crunched under the horses' hoofs. The trail wound along a high bench among spruce trees. The pungence of spruce scent filled the cold air. Then we dropped into muskeg country. There were beaver-dammed creeks, and ponds of slick ice. Mile after mile the horses lunged through half-frozen muck and water. In the fresh snow we saw the tracks of a pack of wolves.

That night the cold, glittering, stars shone through the trees as we rode through the stunted arctic spruce forest. We came to another wild meadow, and camped by an old trapper's cache. While I cooked sup-per, Ruth and Lucky battled over blowing up an air mattress. When it was half-filled, Ruth was blowing hard. Lucky made a running leap on the mattress, forcing the air back into Ruth's cheeks. They continued to battle until I called them to supper.

The trail was pure torture the next day. Time and again Harry or Lucky called back for us to get off and walk. Once we came to a deep ravine, filled with muddy water. Lucky and the hunters had crossed. Harry, Ruth, and I had to switch the packhorses with willows, and we almost had to push them down the steep bank. Finally, they slid down on their haunches, swam across, then lunged and fought their way up the slippery far bank.

All were across but Bunny and Bobo. They stood looking uneasily at the ravine, undecided. We shouted and waved our hats until they too finally took the plunge and swam across, searching for a low place to climb out. Bunny finally made it, but Bobo fell over backward, snort-ing wildly. Ruth and I yelled, trying to encourage her to get out. Ruth was getting ready to leap in when Lucky ran and jumped into the icy and muddy water beside the frightened horse. He grabbed Bobo's halter, pulled her to her feet, and coaxed her up the steep slope. Dripping and shivering, he glared at Ruth. "Stop yelling."

Farther along I rode under a fluttering white piece of paper. I called back, "Ruth, maybe that's a note for us."

She snatched it off and read. "Please get off. 'Nother bad place. Lucky."

I groaned. Ruth snapped, "He can go to the devil. I'm so tired I can't walk another step."

"Me too," I agreed, thinking that the horses always got through. All we had to do was to stick on.

Ruth rode ahead. She turned in the saddle to call back, "What's all that banging and crashing noise?"

"RUTH LOOK OUT!" I yelled.

"E-E-E-EEK!" she screeched, grabbing for leather, as she and Bobo disappeared over the edge.

It was too late for me to stop Bunny. Before we started to slide, ahead I saw a packhorse plummeting down the steep, ice-sheeted trail. Halfway down a huge spruce blocked the trail, and the trail made a sharp turn left. The packhorse crashed into the tree. This turned the horse around, and it sped down the trail backward.

Ruth's Bobo slid down the trail on his haunches, with Ruth struggling to jump off. Too late. Bobo crashed into the tree. Ruth flew from the saddle.

It was impossible for me to jump, and I drew my right leg back so it wouldn't be crushed when Bunny hit the tree. As Bunny slammed into the tree I screamed and flew through the air and slammed into the ground and rolled down the trail. I lay stunned. I felt sick. When I had yelled, my bridge had flown from my mouth. My tongue felt a big gap. Ruth crawled to me, "Dolores, Dolores!" she moaned.

"I could just die," I lisped.

"Where are you hurt?"

"Hurt? I wish I were dead. I lost my tooth. I can't let Louis see me with a big hole in the front of my mouth."

Lucky scrambled up the trail. He was furious. "You kill yourselves. Louie kill me. When Harry'n me say walk, GET OFF HORSE! Understand?"

Ruth pulled me to my feet and Lucky snapped, "Long way yet to camp. Better hurry."

"I'm not leaving until I find my tooth!" I yelled.

Harry and the outfit were waiting at the bottom of the steep hill. Ruth hurriedly explained about my tooth to Lucky. He yelled down to Harry. "Come up. Help us find somep'n lost."

As the four of us crawled around on our knees searching for my tooth, I was so humiliated I cried.

"What look like?" Harry asked.

"Look for gold," I lisped, trying to talk with my mouth shut.

"Gold!" Lucky giggled. "Big stampede." And he scratched over the snow.

"Mrs. Brown, where you when come out?" Lucky asked.

I pointed.

"Lie same place," Harry grunted.

I sprawled in the muck and they tried to figure out how far a chunk of gold would soar. It looked hopeless. The horses were getting restless, and the hunters were having a hard time holding them. The sun had set, and it was dark in the heavy timber.

Harry lit his cigarette lighter, and the small flame moved slowly over the trail. Suddenly, Harry stood up with a broad grin, and placed the icy tooth in my hand! I almost threw my arms around him.

In another hour of travel, out of the darkness loomed an old two-story cabin, half fallen in. It was an old roadhouse, the remnants of a gold-rusher's dream. Ruth and I tore timber from the rotting building, and built a fire. We were numb with cold. We tried to get both front and back warm at the same time, while we looked longingly at the hunter's tent with its warm spiral of smoke pouring from the squatty stovepipe.

That night we made our bed under the eaves of the old roadhouse. In the moonlight, each willow leaf sparkled with frost. As we grew warm and drowsy, Ruth sighed, "This has been the most wonderful summer of my life."

Trail's End

We spent two more nights on the trail. From our last camp we heard the big compressors of the United Keno Silver Mines, and watched the twinkle of the camp's electric lights. Civilization. I could hardly wait to see Louis. If I had had my way, I would have ridden all night. As Ruth and I lay warm between our two bear hides, I wondered aloud, "Do you suppose Louis can walk without crutches? Do you suppose his leg and arm have healed? I wonder if he's all right?"

"Of course he is," Ruth said, trying to quiet my fears. "If Mr. Reynolds has brought my car to Keno we'll drive to your ranch as soon as we get in."

The night was pitch black when we rode into Keno. Lucky and Harry were to stay with the hunters at the Silver Queen hotel that night. We planned for Louis to drive in the next day to pick them up. We found Ruth's car where Mr. Reynolds had promised to leave it. As we climbed in, Lucky jumped into the back seat.

"Lucky, you're supposed to stay with the hunters," I said.

"Gotta see Louie," he said, refusing to get out.

"I wonder if I've forgotten how to drive," Ruth said. "The car feels strange."

As we started down the narrow road, I yelled, "Ruth, don't go so fast!"

"But Dolores, I'm only going 20 miles an hour."

"That's 15 miles an hour faster than Bunny. This speed scares me stiff."

Lucky, in the back seat, softly strummed his guitar and hummed. "Go'n sing new hunt'n song for Louie."

Later, in a serious voice, he asked, "My friend Ruth, how you get married?"

"By a minister, of course," she replied. "I hope to get married in a civilized way. I hope you'll get married in a civilized way," she said, stiffly.

"Lucky not dumb," the young wrangler informed her.

We sped down the winding road under a spectacular display of northern lights, while Lucky labored over his hunting song. My heart began to race as Ruth turned off the highway and onto the narrow old wood road that led to the ranch. We came around a bend, and there stood our little log cabin in the middle of the clearing.

"Stop, Ruth," said Lucky.

We all got out and took care to not slam the doors. We quietly walked across the field and stood before the door. Lucky had planned a big entrance. All was quiet. Lucky's fingers swept across the strings, and he burst into song.

"Back from *Neechemoos*, hunt'n fair

Got lots sheep, caribou, and bear."

I could stand it no longer. I opened the door, laughing. Louis' voice came to me out of the darkness. "Dolores! You're back!"

I ran to the bed and threw my arms about him and he held me close. "Thank God you're back. I'll never let you go again."

Then the four of us were laughing and talking. Lucky lit a candle. Louis looked like a stranger—I had never seen him with whiskers. Embarrassed, he rubbed his hand over his face. "I was going to shave, but I didn't expect you for several days."

Then Lucky told him about the hunters, and how they expected to hunt moose on and around the ranch. "I'll finish the hunt with them," Louis said.

Louis dressed while Lucky nervously paced the floor.

"Got anything to eat?" Lucky asked.

"Sure. A whole moose," Louis said, proudly. Then he showed us row after row of canned meat. "And I saved a hindquarter so we could have a little fresh meat this winter," he said.

"Louis, you're a wonderful hunter," I praised.

Lucky glared. "Mrs. Brown forget Lucky good hunter, too."

"Lucky, would you hunt with a heavy cast on your leg and arm?" I asked.

He hung his head. "No, Mrs. Brown. Louie best hunter."

In a babble, Lucky, Ruth, and I tried to tell Louis all about the hunt. He kept shaking his head and muttering that it was a wonder we had all returned alive. I had a difficult time convincing Louis that our three hunter/clients had collected two sheep, three caribou, three grizzly bears, a wolf, and one moose. And, in addition, in protection of self and property I had killed one black and one grizzly bear.

At last Lucky stood and reminded us that in four hours our hunters would be ready to go on their moose hunt. Ruth and Lucky left to return to Mayo. Lucky planned to catch a ride to Carmacks to see his Mary, and Ruth had to catch a plane to attend a teachers' convention. As soon as we were alone, Louis said, happily, "I kept your silver tea set polished."

Sure enough, the silver service gleamed in the candlelight. Somehow, though, it wasn't important. Somehow, I had changed. I knew for sure that I would never again cower in the cabin when I heard a wolf howl. Likely, I thought, smiling to myself, I'd step outside and plug the varmint for disturbing my sleep.

Louis, still on crutches, found a bull moose for Mr. Miller to shoot. They left, delighted with their adventures and with their wonderful trophies.

I had a few trophies, too. They were memory trophies of a marvelous valley, filled with beauty and peace, memories of a cocky young Indian who worked his heart out to please, and who, in doing so, had grown in many ways. They were memories of a faithful Indian guide, who, for his friend Louis, took orders from a White Squaw for more than a month, and who used his great skill as a hunter to please three clients.

*   *   *

A few weeks later the door of our cabin silently opened behind me, and a current copy of *The Whitehorse Star* was flung onto the table. I looked up to see Lucky. He stood beside the door, tall now, and somehow older. He was resplendent in a new beaded caribou skin jacket. He straddled a chair.

"Lucky get married by minister," he announced, jabbing his finger at an item in the newspaper to prove it.

"Congratulations, Lucky. I wish you every happiness," I said, stretching my hand to shake his.

Lucky ignored my hand and fumbled at the strings of a package. "Bring you'n Louie wedding present."

"But Lucky. It's we who give you a gift. You don't have to give us presents."

"OK. What you give Lucky?"

"Why, Louis and I haven't decided."

"Better be good. Lucky go lots bother get married." Then he added, accusingly, "Mrs. Brown, you not tell Lucky cost lots money get married. Lucky broke."

Louis swung into the room from outside, skillfully working his crutches. He grinned at Lucky. "You look like a bridegroom."

Embarrassed, Lucky grabbed for the package. "Mrs. Brown, shut eyes."

I felt a hat jammed down on my head. Lucky said, "Cost lots money. That 5X beaver felt."

Lucky had hated my old hat. I removed from my head the lovely cowgirl hat he had brought me, and I admired it long and lavishly. It was beautiful, and I loved it. Lucky couldn't know that I would treasure that hat for more than its intrinsic value—I would treasure it as a gift from a faithful wrangler who had ridden with me on a long, tough trail.

Lucky then handed Louis a pair of cowboy boots. How he knew the proper size I never learned, but when Louis tossed away his crutches and could walk again, they were a perfect fit. They too were expensive. Lucky had blown a pile for our gifts—a measure of his regard for us.

"Now, what you give Lucky?" he asked.

Louis and I looked at each other. Louis said, "Lucky, I can't get over how much you've grown on this hunt. You're several inches taller, I believe, and you've put on weight."

Lucky snickered. "Weigh about 200 now."

Dripping wet, he might have weighed 120 pounds.

Louis smiled, "When you and Copper started on the hunting trail you were both colts. Now he's a horse, and you're a man. You've grown together. You belong to each other. Copper is our wedding present to you."

With a wild whoop, Lucky shot out the door and I heard his familiar whistle. Copper came galloping, and the two stood together at the cabin door, Lucky with his arm over the horse. I found a blue hair ribbon and tied it to Copper's forelock, explaining to Lucky, "At weddings, blue is for good luck."

Lucky turned his head and buried it in Copper's mane. When he turned back to look at us, his eyes were glistening.

Editor's Note

Dolores Cline Brown learned to love the wilderness from her uncle, W. T. Wooten, a Game Protector in Columbia County, Washington. When Wooten died, Dolores, a resident of Washington state, made up her mind to find a real wilderness. She went on a big game hunt in the Yukon Territory, where, in addition to big game, she found a husband. In 1953 she married Louis Brown, her Yukon guide. The Browns were married in the historical log church in Whitehorse where famed goldrush poet Robert Service was an elder.

Louis Brown, born in Alberta, arrived at Dawson City, Yukon, in 1934, and started guiding hunters in 1947. He raised registered Scotch Highland cattle, and was a successful prospecter who sold some of his mineral finds to mining companies.

Dolores followed her husband on trophy trails in the wilderness of Canada's Yukon Territory for nearly 20 years. In those years she held both outfitter and guide licenses for the Yukon.

Louis died in 1987. Dolores now divides her time between her ranch near Mayo where she and Louis lived, her home at McQuestion Lake, and an apartment in Mayo. She says the kindness and help of her Indian friends helped her to survive after Louis died.

Other books written by Dolores Brown include *Yukon Trophy Trails*, and *Bonnet Plume's Gold*. She has also written many magazine articles about the Yukon.